THE COOKIE DOCTOR®
Cookbook

Countless Combinations of Delicious Meals
for Any Calorie-Controlled Lifestyle

SANFORD SIEGAL, D.O., M.D.

⊠EGG&DART™

Published by Egg & Dart™, a division of Dynamic Housewares Inc
Copyright 2010 by Dynamic Housewares Inc

Dr. Siegal's Cookie Diet® is a registered trademark of SM Licensing Corp.

10 9 8 7 6 5 4 3 2 1

First paperback edition 2010

This book is not intended as a medical manual. It is not intended to be used to diagnose or treat any medical condition or disease. You should consult your doctor before starting any weight-loss program or making any changes to your diet.

To make this book more readable, the use of trademark symbols (™ and ®) to identify intellectual property has been avoided in most cases. Dr. Siegal's®, Dr. Siegal's Cookie Diet®, Cookie Doctor®, and the name and likeness of Dr. Sanford Siegal are trademarks of SM Licensing Corporation. All other trademarks and registered trademarks mentioned in this book, including those of brand name products, are the property of their respective owners.

Author:
Sanford Siegal, D.O., M.D.

Book Design and Food Photographs:
Christian and Elise Stella

Copy Editor: Kelly Machamer

Manufactured in the USA

ISBN 978-0-9841887-6-5

CONTENTS

INTRODUCTION

FROM COOKIE TO COOKBOOK

This cookbook is long overdue. As the creator of Dr. Siegal's Cookie Diet, a well-known weight-loss approach that's been around for more than 35 years, I've been asked the same question countless times by people who approach me in public: "What should I eat to lose (or maintain) weight?" Surely, this cookbook will answer the question more completely than I can during short exchanges and chance encounters.

Before we go any further, I want to make it clear that this book is intended for anyone who wishes to reach or maintain a proper weight, regardless of the particular regimen he or she may follow. At the end of the day, achieving and maintaining a healthful weight involves consuming a certain number of calories. The recipes in this book make it easy to regulate your caloric intake.

My name is Sanford Siegal and I am a practicing physician in Miami, Florida. I have exclusively treated overweight patients for more than fifty years. Although I discovered early in my career that I had a knack for helping my patients lose weight, for the first fifteen or so years, I was dissatisfied with the results I was getting. My success rate with patients was as good as any doctor's at the time, which was not very good. The problem, I knew, was hunger. If my patients stuck to a reduced-calorie diet, they lost weight, but too many couldn't stick to it because they were simply too hungry.

In the early 1970s, I was writing a book about why certain foods (or, to be more precise, certain components of foods) seem to satisfy hunger better than others. It was already generally accepted that proteins do the job better than carbohydrates and that sugars, in fact, can actually stimulate hunger. In the course of writing my book, I came up with the idea of trying to create an ideal food for satisfying hunger. In other words, I decided to engineer a food that contained a particular spectrum of amino acids (the building blocks of protein) that I found to be particularly good at satisfying my hunger and that of an informal group of test subjects (friends, family, and office staff).

My purpose in creating a hunger-satisfying food was to enable my patients to follow a reduced-calorie diet without becoming so hungry that they gave up. After several years of experimentation in my home kitchen, I came up with a formula of amino acids that I hoped would be useful to my patients. Once I had my formula, I needed a food in which to put it. I chose a cookie because

it seemed like an ideal vehicle. It was small, portable, didn't need refrigeration, and, of course, just about everyone likes cookies.

In 1975, I selected a small group of patients and put them on a new diet. During the day, they were to eat six cookies (that I baked myself at home) and then have a dinner consisting of around 500 calories (depending on the patient) from good, healthy sources. I instructed them not to eat the cookies at set times but rather when they were truly hungry. My hope was that the cookies would take the edge off of my patients' hunger until dinner and that, ultimately, they'd be able to stick to a reduced-calorie diet until they reached their goal.

As you probably know, Dr. Siegal's Cookie Diet was an enormous success. My patients loved it. Within two years, my practice had exploded and doctors were calling me from across the country. By the 1980s, I was supplying my cookies to physicians around the United States, and the media and the public were referring to me as "The Cookie Doctor."

In 2007, I teamed up with my son Matthew to take Dr. Siegal's Cookie Diet products directly to the public through a web site and retail stores. The launch of www.CookieDiet.com and the opening of our Beverly Hills

Josie Raper, before and after losing 120 pounds on Dr. Siegal's Cookie Diet!

store brought massive media attention that continues to this day. Seemingly overnight, everyone was talking about my cookies. Reports of celebrity fans began popping up. We were on Good Morning America, The Today Show, Entertainment Tonight, The View, and many other shows.

With the truly inspiring weight loss story of Josie Raper we even made the cover of People magazine. A 29 year-old mother from Arizona, she lost half of her body weight — an amazing 120 pounds— in just six months on Dr Siegal's Cookie Diet.

Dr. Siegal's Cookie Diet cookies have become a phenomenon because they're simple and convenient, and they taste good. Notice that I didn't say "great" or "delicious" or "amazing." I worked very hard to make my cookies taste the way they do: good, but not too good. Having access to a limitless supply of tempting junk food has made the majority of us overweight and that's not what Dr. Siegal's Cookie Diet cookies are about. My cookies are intended to be used in place of other foods that are higher in calories and fat. Whether you're trying to lose weight, maintain your current weight, or simply satisfy your hunger with a tasty snack, my cookies are an excellent choice. The successes I've seen are greater and more inspiring than I

Marty Moorehead, before and after losing 164 pounds on Dr. Siegal's Cookie Diet!

could have ever hoped for.

Stories like that of Marty Moorehead—who lost 164 pounds and went from a 56 inch waist, down to a size 38—show the unwavering determination of amazing people who were able to utilize my diet to achieve such astounding results.

My first goal in writing this cookbook was to answer all of my patients and dieters' requests for help in choosing the right meals to make on Dr. Siegal's Cookie Diet. I wanted to create a book that made preparing a healthy meal that fits into your daily calorie allowance just as effortless as the rest of the diet. Upon embarking on this project, it became very evident that this book could not only help those on Dr. Siegal's Cookie Diet, but anyone on any restricted calorie diet that is looking for hearty meals with a high level of versatility. In fact, the recipes in this book are so satisfying and delicious that they can most certainly be appreciated by just about anyone, calorie conscious or not!

This book provides 120 recipes and is divided into sections based on calories of 100, 200, 300, 400, and 500. This arrangement gives you the greatest flexibility in adhering to a set calorie lifestyle. Whether your goal is to lose or maintain weight, it is your daily caloric intake that will determine if you succeed or fail. Unfortunately, accurately gauging your calories is a lot harder than you may think, especially if you eat in restaurants. Plenty of innocent looking restaurant dishes are actually loaded with fat that you can't see. By providing a selection of snacks and meals that you can create at home, this book enables you to combine recipes to achieve the daily calorie totals you desire.

Unlike other low-calorie cookbooks, this book is not only about the amount of calories, but also where the calories come from. Most low-calorie cookbooks available today focus only on the number of calories in the recipe and have little regard for the amount of protein, fiber, or carbohydrates included in those calories. Just as I strived to create a hunger-satisfying cookie to get you through the day, I've strived to make the recipes in this book as satiating as possible to keep your weight loss on track. Though I was hesitant to create a book of such delicious recipes at first—as I do not want to encourage the overeating that can lead to obesity—I am now quite confident that the high fiber and protein content of my recipes will satisfy you without the need to overeat. Not to mention, because I am using healthy, low-calorie ingredients, the serving sizes of my recipes are extremely generous— the most realistically satisfying portion

sizes I've seen in any low-calorie cookbook. While most low-calorie cookbooks consider 4 ounces to be a normal portion of chicken breast, my chicken breast recipes usually include double that (8 ounces, or 1/2 pound) per serving. Chicken breast is naturally low in calories and fat and high in the protein you need to feel full—no recipe should limit it just to make room for less important calories!

On Dr. Siegal's Cookie Diet, I recommend a dinner of 500-700 calories, depending on your weight loss needs. I can promise you that if you combine recipes in this book to form a 500-700 calorie meal, you will NOT need to overeat to feel satisfied. Which brings me to what may be the most important thing about this book: the grouping of recipes by calories.

I have arranged this book to be one of the easiest to follow and most versatile low-calorie cookbooks ever written. Whether you are using Dr. Siegal's Cookie Diet cookies to achieve your goal or are on another low-calorie diet, you should have a set amount of calories that you need to stay at or under to lose weight. By arranging my recipes by their calories per serving, I am allowing you to easily find and combine recipes into YOUR perfect meal for YOUR necessary calorie allowance.

There are literally thousands of ways that you can mix and match the recipes in this book to create a 500 calorie meal, including the easiest—the 500 Calorie section itself—which is comprised entirely of recipes that are already complete meals (as I realize that a good majority of people will not have any calories over that amount to add on vegetables, etc.).

There is a chart at the end of this section that illustrates the idea of mixing and matching the recipes in this book better than I can explain it. While the chart shows many different ways to create a 500 calorie meal, I am confident that this book can be used to create a full and satisfying meal in as little as 300 calories. On the other end of the spectrum, there are absolutely endless ways to create a 700 calorie meal.

I have tried to keep the recipes in this book as close to the calorie amount of the section that they are in, but as you may find, some recipes go over the amount (by no more than 45 calories) and other recipes will go under the amount of calories (again, by no more than 45 calories).

Nutritional information is for one serving of each recipe and has been calculated using sophisticated software that is as accurate as we can obtain. However, it is important to note that different brands of similar food ingredients do vary in calorie and nutritional content, so you should always shop smart! Read nutritional labels and make informed decisions about the foods you purchase.

I'm confident you will find this book useful in achieving your goals, both short term (What's for dinner?) and well into the long term of maintaining a healthy, normal weight.

I wish you well, and bon appétit!

Sanford Siegal, D.O., M.D.
The Cookie Doctor®
Miami, Florida

My son, Matthew, and I.

JUST SOME OF THE THOUSANDS OF WAYS TO MAKE A 500 CALORIE MEAL !

 500 CALORIES

 400 CALORIES +  100 CALORIES

 300 CALORIES +  200 CALORIES

 300 CALORIES +  100 CALORIES +  100 CALORIES

 200 CALORIES ×  2 PORTIONS +  100 CALORIES

 100 CALORIES ×  4 PORTIONS +  100 CALORIES

Chicken Piccata
Mandarin Orange Salad
Maple Glazed Salmon
400°
Bake 15-20 min

100 calories

CALORIES	FAT	PROTEIN	CARBS	FIBER
125	1g	6g	24g	2g

BAKED AND NOT FRIED GREEN TOMATOES

PREP TIME: 20 MINS   COOK TIME: 22 MINS   SERVES: 4

Fried green tomatoes are one of those great southern side dishes that you may have had at a little diner off of a highway at some point in your life. Made from green, unripe tomatoes breaded with cornmeal, the typical preparation involves deep frying, but I say bake them! While I can't promise that these are as crunchy as the deep fried diner variety, I can promise that they have only 1 gram of fat—a trade-off that is more than worth it.

SHOPPING LIST

nonstick cooking spray

4 green tomatoes

2 large egg whites

½ cup buttermilk

¼ cup water

¾ cup all-purpose flour

¼ cup cornmeal

¼ teaspoon onion powder

¼ teaspoon salt

¼ teaspoon pepper

1 Preheat oven to 400 degrees F. Spray a sheet pan with nonstick cooking spray.

2 Slice ends off green tomatoes and discard. Slice the trimmed tomatoes into ¼ inch thick slices.

3 In a mixing bowl, whisk together egg whites, buttermilk, and water. In a separate bowl, combine flour, cornmeal, onion powder, salt, and pepper.

4 Double-bread each tomato slice by first dipping into the egg mixture, then the flour mixture, then repeating. Place onto the greased sheet pan as you go, arranging all breaded tomato slices in a single layer.

5 Bake 10 minutes, flip, and then bake an additional 8-12 minutes, or until tomato slices are lightly browned. Serve hot.

DR. SIEGAL'S TIPS

If desired (and if allowed in your diet), sprinkle lightly with additional salt as soon as you remove the baked tomatoes from the oven.

100 calories

CALORIES	FAT	PROTEIN	CARBS	FIBER
85	2g	15g	1.5g	0g

CRAB STUFFED DEVILED EGGS

PREP TIME: 25 MINS   COOK TIME: 0 MINS   SERVES: 4

Deviled eggs are one of the perfect cocktail party dishes, but their egg yolk filling is loaded with cholesterol. This recipe is the perfect alternative, as it is not only healthier but even fancier than ordinary deviled eggs! While crab meat also has some cholesterol, it is nearly 4 times less than that of the egg yolk it replaces! With a serving of 4 deviled egg halves coming in at only 85 calories, this is one party food you can feel good about indulging in.

SHOPPING LIST

8 hardboiled eggs, chilled
1 cup canned crab meat, drained
3 tablespoons light mayonnaise
1 teaspoon Dijon mustard
2 tablespoons diced pimento
½ teaspoon Old Bay seasoning
⅛ teaspoon onion powder
chopped fresh parsley for garnish

1 Peel and slice hardboiled eggs in half lengthwise. Scoop out and discard yolks.

2 In a mixing bowl, combine all remaining ingredients, except parsley, tossing gently until mixed.

3 Fill each hardboiled egg white half with a heaping spoonful of the crab filling until all 16 halves are filled.

4 Top each deviled egg with a small pinch of fresh parsley before serving cold.

DR. SIEGAL'S TIPS

I like to prepare hard-boiled eggs by starting with refrigerated eggs in a pot of cold water (with only a pinch of salt) over high heat. I cover the pot, bring it up to a boil, and then turn the heat off completely. Let the pot sit, still covered, for 15 minutes before carefully draining. The eggs should be fully hardboiled.

The closer the eggs are to their sell-by date, the easier the hardboiled eggs will be to peel!

100 calories

CALORIES	FAT	PROTEIN	CARBS	FIBER
105	1g	12g	8g	1.5g

CREAM CHEESE STUFFED MUSHROOMS

PREP TIME: 20 MINS   COOK TIME: 15 MINS   SERVES: 4

Cream cheese and chives make a uniquely different filling for this stuffed mushroom recipe. With a serving of about 4 mushrooms per 100 calories, these somehow manage to be both more satisfying and healthier than traditional breadcrumb-only stuffed mushrooms.

100 calories

SHOPPING LIST

nonstick cooking spray

1 pound button mushrooms, stems removed

8 ounces fat-free cream cheese

1 tablespoon chopped chives

¼ teaspoon salt

⅛ teaspoon pepper

2 tablespoons Italian breadcrumbs

1 tablespoon Parmesan cheese

1 Preheat oven to 375 degrees F. Spray a sheet pan with nonstick cooking spray and arrange mushroom caps, tops down.

2 In a food processor, pulse cream cheese, chives, salt, and pepper until well combined.

3 Fill each mushroom cap with an even amount of the cream cheese mixture.

4 Combine breadcrumbs and Parmesan cheese, and sprinkle over top all stuffed mushrooms.

5 Bake 12-15 minutes, or until mushrooms are tender and filling is hot. Serve immediately.

DR. SIEGAL'S TIPS

You don't need to use the food processor in step 2 if you let the cream cheese soften on the counter and then mix it into the other ingredients by hand with a very sturdy spoon. I sometimes find that easier than cleaning out the processor!

CALORIES	FAT	PROTEIN	CARBS	FIBER
90	4g	5.5g	7g	1.5g

CLAMS IN RED SAUCE

PREP TIME: 15 MINS   COOK TIME: 15 MINS   SERVES: 4

This family-style appetizer of clams in a stewed tomato, onion, and pepper sauce would even make a great entrée in larger portions. At only 90 calories per serving, you could eat the entire dish for an entrée of only 360 calories. With a recipe this fresh and delicious, you may just want to!

SHOPPING LIST

2 pounds fresh clams

1 tablespoon olive oil

½ of 1 red onion, diced

1 small green bell pepper, diced

2 stalks celery, diced

2 cloves garlic, crushed

1 (10-ounce) can diced tomatoes with green chilies

3 tablespoons dry white wine

¼ teaspoon salt

⅛ teaspoon pepper

1 Scrub clams well to remove any grit.

2 Place olive oil, red onion, bell pepper, celery, and garlic in a large nonstick skillet over medium-high heat and sauté until vegetables are soft, about 6 minutes.

3 Add diced tomatoes, white wine, salt, pepper, and scrubbed clams. Cover skillet and let simmer 6-10 minutes, or until all of the clams are open. Serve immediately, smothered in sauce from the pan.

DR. SIEGAL'S TIPS

If most clams have opened and there are just a few stragglers refusing to open, this is a good indication that those clams are no good and need to be discarded before serving.

100 calories

CALORIES	FAT	PROTEIN	CARBS	FIBER
130	6.5g	15g	3g	0.5g

TOMATO AND BASIL OMELET

PREP TIME: 10 MINS   COOK TIME: 5 MINS   SERVES: 1

It's no secret that egg whites are a surefire favorite of mine, especially when used to make egg white omelets. This particular omelet is one that I make quite often—as it is simple, fresh, and as low in calories as it gets! With tomatoes, basil, and Parmesan cheese, I'm sure that they would love this in Italy, but I'm not sure that they even eat omelets there!

SHOPPING LIST

2 teaspoons light (and trans-fat free) margarine

salt and pepper

3 large egg whites

2 tablespoons shredded Parmesan cheese

3 slices tomato

2 leaves basil, chopped

1 Melt margarine in a medium-sized nonstick skillet over medium heat.

2 Whisk a pinch of salt and pepper into the egg whites, and pour into the skillet. Let cook 2-3 minutes, or until slightly set.

3 Once the egg is slightly set, sprinkle Parmesan cheese over top all. Fan the 3 slices of tomato out over only ½ of the egg, leaving the other half bare (to fold over). Sprinkle the chopped basil over top of the tomatoes.

4 Once the egg is almost entirely set, use a spatula to fold the egg over and form the omelet.

5 Transfer to a plate and serve garnished with fresh basil.

DR. SIEGAL'S TIPS

3 tablespoons of shredded mozzarella or crumbled feta cheese can be used in place of the Parmesan but will raise the calorie count by about 30 calories.

100 calories

CALORIES	FAT	PROTEIN	CARBS	FIBER
115	1g	6g	20g	4.5g

CRUNCHY RANCH CHICKPEAS

PREP TIME: 10 MINS   COOK TIME: 35 MINS   SERVES: 4

Chickpeas (also known as garbanzo beans) are a great source of protein and fiber and have almost as much calcium as milk! While they are often smashed into creamy hummus spreads, this recipe takes the opposite approach; it roasts them until they are dry and crunchy, almost like a half-popped popcorn kernel. Seasoning them with powdered ranch salad dressing mix makes them irresistible, but feel free to create your own flavor combinations!

SHOPPING LIST

nonstick cooking spray

1 (15-ounce) can chickpeas

powdered ranch salad dressing mix, to taste

1 Preheat oven to 375 degrees F. Spray a sheet pan with nonstick cooking spray.

2 Drain the chickpeas extremely well and then wrap them in paper towels to soak up any remaining moisture. Spread chickpeas out in a single layer on the sheet pan.

3 Bake 20 minutes at 375 degrees F., and then shake the sheet pan to rotate chickpeas.

4 Return chickpeas to the oven and raise the oven temperature to 425 degrees F. (Do not worry about preheating; just leave them in as the temperature rises.) Bake for 10-20 additional minutes, or until chickpeas look golden brown and somewhat shriveled.

5 Remove from oven and sprinkle with powdered ranch mix to taste. Shake the pan to coat all sides with the ranch powder. Let cool at least 5 minutes before eating.

DR. SIEGAL'S TIPS

I only recommend using 1-2 teaspoons of the ranch seasoning as it is very high in sodium. If you are concerned about sodium, or would just like to try something different, you can also make these with curry powder.

WEDGE SALAD WITH BLUE CHEESE DRESSING

PREP TIME: 15 MINS   COOK TIME: 5 MINS   SERVES: 4

Wedge salads, like those that you can get at almost any steakhouse, are a simple and unique way to start a meal. Typically, they are extremely high in fat, as they are not only topped with chopped bacon but smothered in a high-fat blue cheese dressing. My recipe includes a delicious blue cheese dressing that is extremely low in fat and far better tasting than low-fat dressings sold in stores.

SHOPPING LIST

4 slices turkey bacon, chopped
1 small head lettuce, quartered
⅔ cup grape tomatoes, halved
2 green onions, sliced

DRESSING

¼ cup fat-free mayonnaise
⅓ cup fat-free evaporated milk
⅛ teaspoon garlic powder
¼ teaspoon Worcestershire sauce
⅛ teaspoon salt
⅛ teaspoon pepper
¼ cup crumbled blue cheese

1 Place the chopped turkey bacon in a skillet over medium-high heat. Sauté until well browned, about 5 minutes. Transfer to a small dish and refrigerate until chilled, about 10 minutes.

2 Arrange the 4 wedges of iceberg lettuce on 4 serving plates. Sprinkle evenly with the grape tomatoes and green onions.

3 Pour an equal amount of the blue cheese dressing over top all and serve.

BLUE CHEESE DRESSING

In a mixing bowl, whisk together all dressing ingredients except crumbled blue cheese. Gently fold in blue cheese, cover, and refrigerate for 30 minutes to let the flavors combine before serving.

The dressing may thin out if refrigerated overnight.

100 calories

CALORIES	FAT	PROTEIN	CARBS	FIBER
75	3.5g	2g	9g	3g

SPINACH SALAD WITH PEARS

PREP TIME: 15 MINS   COOK TIME: 0 MINS   SERVES: 4

Nutritionally, raw spinach is far superior to ordinary lettuce, but that isn't the only reason why this salad is great! The combination of spinach, pears, and walnut oil in the dressing makes for a light and fruity but very earthy flavor that—at under 100 calories—you can eat guilt free. The dressing packs a powerful punch, so a little goes a long way, which helps keep this recipe light.

SHOPPING LIST

8 ounces fresh spinach

¼ red onion, thinly sliced

1 pear, cored and sliced thin

DRESSING

3 tablespoons balsamic vinegar

2 teaspoons Dijon mustard

1 ½ tablespoons water

1 teaspoon honey

⅛ teaspoon salt

⅛ teaspoon pepper

1 tablespoon walnut oil (may use olive oil)

1 Split the spinach equally between 4 bowls.

2 Top the spinach in each bowl with a few slices of red onion, and then fan a few slices of pear across the center of each salad.

3 Create the dressing by adding balsamic vinegar, Dijon mustard, water, honey, salt, and pepper to a blender. Blend until combined.

4 Slowly add walnut oil to dressing, blending as you go, until all is combined. Drizzle over salads and serve.

DR. SIEGAL'S TIPS

The walnut oil really makes this dressing shine, but it may be tough to find. You can usually find it in the oil section of your regular grocery store (near sunflower or other unique oils). Occasionally, it is kept in the organic or health food section of the store.

If you have extra calories available in your daily allowance, add a few chopped walnuts to the salads for a nice crunch!

100 calories

CALORIES	FAT	PROTEIN	CARBS	FIBER
115	7g	4g	10g	3g

Tomato and Gorgonzola Salad

PREP TIME: 15 MINS   COOK TIME: 3 MINS   SERVES: 4

There are so many gorgeous varieties of tomatoes offered in the grocery stores these days, but it isn't always easy to find a recipe that can showcase them. While this recipe for a simple and fresh tomato salad suggests the use of a few types, feel free to use a mixture of any tomatoes you wish.

Shopping List

¼ cup balsamic vinegar

2 tomatoes, halved and sliced

2 yellow tomatoes, halved and sliced

1 pint cherry tomatoes, halved

½ red onion, thinly sliced

6 basil leaves, thinly sliced

¼ cup crumbled gorgonzola cheese

1 tablespoon olive oil

kosher (or coarse) salt and pepper

1 Place the balsamic vinegar in a small saucepot over medium heat. Simmer for 2-3 minutes, or until reduced by half. Transfer to a small dish and refrigerate until chilled, about 20 minutes.

2 Toss all sliced tomatoes, cherry tomatoes, onion, basil, and gorgonzola cheese until all ingredients are equally dispersed.

3 Arrange the tossed ingredients on a large serving platter. Drizzle with olive oil and the reduced and chilled balsamic vinegar.

4 Sprinkle with a generous amount of kosher salt and black pepper before serving.

Dr. Siegal's Tips

Kosher or coarse sea salt works best with the tomatoes in this recipe, but regular salt will do just fine. Of course, you can also enjoy this without any salt at all if you are watching your salt intake.

Freshly ground black pepper from a pepper mill is definitely recommended as well.

100 calories

CALORIES	FAT	PROTEIN	CARBS	FIBER
70	3.5g	2g	9g	3.5g

GREEN BEAN AND TOMATO SALAD

PREP TIME: 20 MINS   CHILL TIME: 1 HOUR   SERVES: 4

Calorically, green beans are one of the biggest bangs for the buck around. A whole pound of green beans (which is A LOT) is only 140 calories and packs over 15 grams of fiber. For this reason, I love to use green beans in picnic salads like this one as you can indulge in a much larger serving than starchier sides like macaroni or potato salad.

SHOPPING LIST

¾ pound green beans

1 tablespoon olive oil

2 teaspoons red wine vinegar

2 teaspoons Dijon mustard

½ teaspoon sugar

¼ teaspoon salt

⅛ teaspoon pepper

1 cup grape tomatoes, halved

¼ of 1 red onion, thinly sliced

1 Snap ends from green beans and discard. Place in boiling water and boil for 4-5 minutes, or until crisp-tender. Drain and rinse under cool water.

2 In a large bowl, whisk olive oil, red wine vinegar, Dijon mustard, sugar, salt, and pepper until fully combined.

3 Add grape tomatoes, red onion, and the cooked green beans to the bowl and toss until all are coated.

4 Cover and refrigerate for at least 1 hour before serving.

DR. SIEGAL'S TIPS

I like to add cooked and chopped turkey bacon to this recipe… it just goes really well with the green beans and tomatoes. Adding 4 slices will only add 20 calories and ½ gram of fat per serving, which would still keep this recipe under 100 calories!

100 calories

CALORIES	FAT	PROTEIN	CARBS	FIBER
105	3.5g	5g	19g	4.5g

SUMMER SUCCOTASH

PREP TIME: 15 MINS   COOK TIME: 12 MINS   SERVES: 4

Simple vegetable recipes like this one are an integral part of any good home cook's repertoire. Knowing how to throw together a good simple succotash will ensure that your entire meal is interesting and not just the main course. This particular succotash is not your typical frozen lima bean mixture, but instead a much fresher combination full of color and flavor.

SHOPPING LIST

2 tablespoons light (and trans-fat free) margarine

2 zucchini, sliced

2 large yellow squash, sliced

1 cup frozen corn kernels

2 teaspoons lemon juice

2 teaspoons minced garlic

¼ teaspoon Italian seasoning

¼ teaspoon salt

⅛ teaspoon black pepper

1 cup grape tomatoes, halved

1 tablespoon chopped fresh parsley

1 Place margarine in a large skillet over medium heat.

2 Once margarine is sizzling, add the zucchini and yellow squash and sauté 5 minutes.

3 Stir the frozen corn, lemon juice, garlic, Italian seasoning, salt, and pepper into the skillet, cover, and let cook 5 minutes.

4 Add grape tomatoes and chopped parsley, and stir all to combine. Sauté for 1 additional minute before serving.

DR. SIEGAL'S TIPS

I like to cut the zucchini and yellow squash into discs about ¼ inch thick and then cut those discs into quarters as seen in the picture on page: 108.

100 calories

CALORIES	FAT	PROTEIN	CARBS	FIBER
80	5g	2g	8g	4g

CHAR-BROILED GREEN BEANS

PREP TIME: 10 MINS   COOK TIME: 8 MINS   SERVES: 4

This is one of those recipes that may eventually have you thinking, why didn't I think of that? Using the broiler to literally char fresh green beans until they are nicely browned might not sound good at first, but I promise that these are positively delicious, with an almost nutty taste. Much like roasting garlic or peppers brings out all kinds of great flavors, the same can now be said for green beans!

100 calories

SHOPPING LIST

1 pound fresh green beans, trimmed or untrimmed

1 ½ tablespoons olive oil

¼ teaspoon onion powder

⅛ teaspoon garlic powder

¼ teaspoon salt

⅛ teaspoon pepper

1 Place the oven rack in its highest position and preheat the broiler to low.

2 In a large mixing bowl, combine all ingredients, tossing until green beans are fully coated in the oil and seasonings.

3 Spread the coated green beans out in a single layer across the surface of a sheet pan and place under the broiler.

4 Broil for 5-8 minutes, removing from the oven and shaking pan to keep them moving at least once. Beans are done when they are a nice, dark brown color on at least 1 side. Serve hot.

DR. SIEGAL'S TIPS

As with anytime you use the broiler, you will want to keep a very close eye on these and make sure that they are not getting too charred. You are looking for a deep brown color, not black.

These make an amazing side for sandwiches like my Tuscan Chicken Sandwiches, recipe page: 101.

CALORIES	FAT	PROTEIN	CARBS	FIBER
120	4g	4g	19g	4g

SPAGHETTI SQUASH WITH CRUSHED TOMATOES

PREP TIME: 15 MINS   COOK TIME: 25 MINS   SERVES: 4

A whole spaghetti squash may look like a tough nut to crack, but preparing one can be a lot easier than you would think! While you prepare the crushed tomato sauce topping on the stove, the spaghetti squash itself is actually cooked in the microwave in less than 10 minutes.

SHOPPING LIST

1 tablespoon olive oil

½ cup diced yellow onion

1 (15-ounce) can crushed tomatoes

2 tablespoons tomato paste

2 teaspoons minced garlic

1 teaspoon Italian seasoning

1 spaghetti squash

salt and pepper

1 Place olive oil and yellow onion in a sauce pot over medium-high heat and sauté until onions are translucent, about 3 minutes.

2 Add crushed tomatoes, tomato paste, minced garlic, and Italian seasoning to the pot and bring up to a simmer. Reduce heat to low and let simmer for 15 minutes.

3 Meanwhile, slice the spaghetti squash in half lengthwise and remove seeds and white membrane. Place the halves facedown in a microwave-safe dish and poke the outer skin with a fork in multiple places. Microwave for about 8 minutes, or until tender.

4 Use a fork to pull the strands of spaghetti squash from the skin.

5 Season the simmered tomato sauce with salt and pepper to taste, and serve over mounds of the spaghetti squash strands.

DR. SIEGAL'S TIPS

I like to serve with a sprinkling of grated Parmesan cheese and fresh chopped parsley.

100 calories

CALORIES	FAT	PROTEIN	CARBS	FIBER
80	3g	5g	8g	1.5g

THE BEST MARINATED MUSHROOMS

PREP TIME: 30 MINS   CHILL TIME: OVERNIGHT   SERVES: 6

Chilled, marinated mushrooms are not only a great snack or appetizer but also make a great side dish for sandwiches like my Tuscan Chicken Sandwiches, recipe page: 101. I make them in a way that I've never seen before, by grilling the mushrooms before marinating! It not only starts to soften the mushrooms, allowing them to marinate faster, but it also adds a great char-grilled flavor to the final result.

SHOPPING LIST

2 pounds small button mushrooms

1 tablespoon olive oil

1 cup fat-free Italian salad dressing

½ cup water

juice of 1 lemon

1 small bunch fresh thyme

2 cloves garlic, sliced

¼ teaspoon pepper

1 Wash all mushrooms and then toss in olive oil.

2 Oil and preheat a grill, indoor grill, or grill pan to high.

3 Place oiled mushrooms on grill and grill only 1-2 minutes, just until grill marks appear. Remove to a large mixing bowl.

4 Cover with all remaining ingredients (leaving the bunch of thyme whole), and stir to combine. Cover and refrigerate overnight before serving chilled. Will keep for up to 2 weeks in the refrigerator.

DR. SIEGAL'S TIPS

Look for "zesty" or "robust" fat-free Italian salad dressing to get the best flavors. These are the types of dressings where you can actually see all the specks of red pepper, garlic, etc. in the bottle.

100 calories

CALORIES	FAT	PROTEIN	CARBS	FIBER
85	4g	5g	8g	3g

SMASHED CAULIFLOWER

PREP TIME: 10 MINS   COOK TIME: 20 MINS   SERVES: 4

Cauliflower is one of the healthiest vegetables on the planet, but other than steaming or boiling it, we don't tend to do much with it! Thankfully "Smashed" Cauliflower has become quite popular and for good reason—it's all the nutrition of cauliflower with the flavor and texture of mashed potatoes.

SHOPPING LIST

1 head cauliflower

2 tablespoons light (and trans-fat free) margarine

½ cup low-fat milk

3 tablespoons grated Parmesan cheese

¼ teaspoon garlic powder

¼ teaspoon salt

⅛ teaspoon pepper

1 tablespoon fresh chopped chives

1 Remove cauliflower florets from the large stem and add florets to a pot of boiling water. Discard stem.

2 Boil cauliflower florets 12-15 minutes, or until completely tender. Drain very well.

3 Place drained cauliflower in a food processor with all remaining ingredients, except chives. Pulse for 1-2 minutes, or until the mixture is smooth and creamy.

4 Transfer to a serving dish and microwave for 1 minute to make sure that it is nice and hot. Stir in chives just before serving.

DR. SIEGAL'S TIPS

You can also use a potato masher to mash the cauliflower instead of a food processor, but it will require a little bit more elbow grease and the final result will not be perfectly smooth.

If the food processor is having trouble smoothing out the cauliflower, you may need to add another tablespoon or two of milk, depending on the size of your head of cauliflower.

100 calories

CALORIES	FAT	PROTEIN	CARBS	FIBER
80	2g	2.5g	14g	3g

BROCCOLI AND RAISIN SLAW

PREP TIME: 10 MINS   CHILL TIME: 1 HOUR   SERVES: 6

I eat broccoli slaw mix in place of a salad all the time. It's sold in the bagged lettuce section of the grocery store, near similar coleslaw mixes. Typically broccoli slaw mix is made up of shoestring cut broccoli stalks, carrots, and red cabbage. This recipe is prepared in a similar fashion as a traditional carrot and raisin salad, but it has a whole lot more nutrition thanks to the high fiber and nutrients found in the broccoli stalks.

100 calories

SHOPPING LIST

¼ cup low-fat mayonnaise

2 tablespoons low-fat milk

2 teaspoons light brown sugar

¼ teaspoon salt

1 (12-ounce) bag shredded broccoli slaw mix

⅓ cup golden raisins

1 In a large bowl, whisk together mayonnaise, milk, brown sugar, and salt, until well combined.

2 Add broccoli slaw mix and raisins to the whisked dressing in the bowl, and stir all to combine.

3 Cover and refrigerate for at least 1 hour before serving.

DR. SIEGAL'S TIPS

You can also make this with fresh broccoli florets in place of the broccoli slaw mix. Simply chop them into small, bite-sized florets for easier mixing. The florets of 1 bunch of broccoli should be just the right amount. You can even slice the stalk of the broccoli and add it as well.

CALORIES	FAT	PROTEIN	CARBS	FIBER
75	2g	5.5g	10g	4g

GREEN BEANS WITH TURKEY BACON

PREP TIME: 15 MINS   COOK TIME: 15 MINS   SERVES: 4

Adding bacon to green beans is a surefire way to have your vegetable dish flying off the table. When it comes to lowering the calories, this simple side has a very simple fix: replacing the regular high-fat bacon with turkey bacon. It cuts the calories in the final dish by more than half!

SHOPPING LIST

4 slices turkey bacon, chopped

½ cup diced red onion

1 pound fresh green beans, ends snapped

1 tablespoon light (and trans-fat free) margarine

2 teaspoons minced garlic

2 teaspoons lemon juice

¼ teaspoon salt

⅛ teaspoon black pepper

1 Place turkey bacon in a large skillet over medium-high heat and cook 2-3 minutes, just until it begins to brown.

2 Add onions to the skillet and cook 3-4 minutes, just until bacon is crispy and onions have softened. Temporarily remove from heat.

3 Meanwhile, add green beans to a large pot of boiling water over high heat, cover, and boil 6-8 minutes, just until crisp-tender.

4 Drain green beans and add to the bacon and onions in skillet. Return to the heat and add all remaining ingredients. Stir constantly to keep the green beans moving, just until margarine has melted and all ingredients have combined. Serve immediately.

DR. SIEGAL'S TIPS

You can also steam the green beans in this recipe in place of boiling them in step 3.

Frozen green beans also work well in this recipe, but nothing beats the snap of a fresh green bean! If you do decide to use frozen, be sure to purchase the fancier, "whole" green beans; they are always of much higher quality than cut beans.

100 calories

CALORIES	FAT	PROTEIN	CARBS	FIBER
80	3g	4g	12g	5g

BRUSSELS SPROUTS WITH CARAMELIZED ONIONS

PREP TIME: 10 MINS   COOK TIME: 20 MINS   SERVES: 4

The natural sweetness that comes out when you caramelize onions really makes them the perfect pair for the nutty flavor of Brussels sprouts. With 5 grams of fiber a serving, Brussels sprouts are one of the healthiest vegetables around. When prepared properly, they are also one of the most delicious vegetables, regardless of what you may have thought as a child!

SHOPPING LIST

2 tablespoons light (and trans-fat free) margarine

1 yellow onion, thinly sliced

1 pound fresh Brussels sprouts, quartered

1 teaspoon minced garlic

¼ teaspoon salt

⅛ teaspoon black pepper

1 Place margarine in a large skillet over medium-high heat.

2 Once margarine is sizzling, add the sliced onions and sauté until they have cooked down and caramelized, about 8-10 minutes.

3 Stir in the Brussels sprouts, minced garlic, salt, pepper, and ⅓ cup of water. Reduce the heat to medium-low, cover, and simmer for 8-10 minutes, or until sprouts are tender. Serve immediately.

DR. SIEGAL'S TIPS

You can also make this recipe with frozen Brussels sprouts with no need to quarter them. Personally, I find frozen Brussels sprouts have an entirely different, stronger flavor than fresh… but they will do if no fresh ones are available.

100 calories

CALORIES	FAT	PROTEIN	CARBS	FIBER
70	2g	2g	8g	3g

ORANGE SNAP PEAS

PREP TIME: 10 MINS   COOK TIME: 5 MINS   SERVES: 4

I absolutely love cooking with all of the wonderful citrus grown in Florida. Orange zest is a wonderfully low-calorie way to add a ton of flavor to good green vegetables like the sugar snap peas in this recipe. In place of salt, low-sodium soy sauce adds a slightly Asian flavor to this snappy side dish.

SHOPPING LIST

1 pound sugar snap peas

1 tablespoon light (and trans-fat free) margarine

2 teaspoons orange zest

2 teaspoons low-sodium soy sauce

⅛ teaspoon garlic powder

⅛ teaspoon pepper

1 Add snap peas to a large pot of boiling water over high heat.

2 Boil snap peas for 2-3 minutes, or until tender but still snappy.

3 Drain and return the snap peas to the pot. Reduce the heat to low and add all remaining ingredients, tossing just until the margarine has melted.

4 Remove from heat and serve immediately.

DR. SIEGAL'S TIPS

You can also prepare this recipe with snow peas, though they cook even faster than snap peas and do not require pre-boiling. Simply sauté them with the remaining ingredients over medium heat for 4-5 minutes.

Frozen snap peas can also be used without pre-boiling in the same method as the tip above.

100 calories

CALORIES	FAT	PROTEIN	CARBS	FIBER
105	5g	5.5g	13g	5g

SESAME BROCCOLI AND BELL PEPPER

PREP TIME: 10 MINS   COOK TIME: 13 MINS   SERVES: 4

Most people do not know that bell peppers are not only mild and delicious, but also packed with antioxidants! The red variety of bell pepper (used in this simple Asian stir fry recipe) is actually far more rich in these antioxidants than green peppers. This is an easy fact to remember, as two of the foods most commonly known for their high antioxidant content just so happen to be red: cranberries and pomegranates.

SHOPPING LIST

2 teaspoons sesame oil

1 tablespoon light (and trans-fat free) margarine

1 large red bell pepper, thinly sliced

florets of 1 bunch broccoli

2 tablespoons reduced-sodium soy sauce

1 teaspoon minced garlic

⅛ teaspoon black pepper

2 teaspoons toasted sesame seeds

1 Place sesame oil, margarine, and red bell peppers in a large skillet over medium-high heat and cook 4-5 minutes, just until bell peppers begin to soften. Temporarily remove from heat.

2 Meanwhile, add broccoli florets to a large pot of boiling water over high heat, cover, and boil 5-6 minutes, just until crisp-tender.

3 Drain broccoli and add to the red bell pepper in skillet. Return to the heat and add all remaining ingredients. Stir constantly to keep the broccoli moving, just until all ingredients are hot and combined. Serve immediately.

DR. SIEGAL'S TIPS

Toasting sesame seeds is easy: Simply place raw sesame seeds in a dry skillet over medium heat and swirl them around the pan until they turn golden brown.

100 calories

CALORIES	FAT	PROTEIN	CARBS	FIBER
90	2g	5.5g	13g	2.5g

ASPARAGUS WITH CREAMY DILL SAUCE

PREP TIME: 15 MINS   COOK TIME: 6 MINS   SERVES: 4

Asparagus has a really great thing going for it—it's green! I say, if it's a green vegetable, eat, eat, and eat some more. Most green vegetables are so low in calories and so high in nutrients that you can simply never have too much! When you want to dress things up a bit, this recipe's creamy dill sauce is a great alternative to higher-fat sauces such as hollandaise.

SHOPPING LIST

1 pound asparagus

8 ounces fat-free sour cream

1 tablespoon low-fat mayonnaise

1 tablespoon low-fat milk

1 tablespoon fresh chopped dill

½ teaspoon lemon juice

⅛ teaspoon garlic powder

⅛ teaspoon salt

⅛ teaspoon black pepper

1 Trim 1-2 inches from the stalks of the asparagus.

2 In a large pot, boil asparagus for 3-6 minutes, or until crisp-tender. Drain well.

3 Meanwhile, in a separate sauce pot over medium heat, bring all remaining ingredients to a simmer, stirring constantly.

4 Serve asparagus drizzled with plenty of the sauce hot off the stove.

DR. SIEGAL'S TIPS

If you have a steamer insert, steaming the asparagus is even better as more of the natural vitamins are retained.

Be sure to carefully pull a stalk of asparagus out of the pot and snap it to test doneness as asparagus can go from crunchy to mushy before you know it, especially if they are pencil thin.

100 calories

CALORIES	FAT	PROTEIN	CARBS	FIBER
120	6.5g	3g	15g	4g

CITRUS GLAZED CARROTS WITH PISTACHIOS

PREP TIME: 10 MINS   COOK TIME: 20 MINS   SERVES: 4

I was going to call this recipe "Orange" Glazed Carrots with Pistachios, but then I realized that you may just pass it over, thinking to yourself, "All carrots are orange!" The zested orange peel in this recipe is a really great addition to traditional glazed carrots, and the chopped pistachios add a nice, nutty crunch that really sets this side dish apart.

100 calories

SHOPPING LIST

2 tablespoons light (and trans-fat free) margarine

1 pound carrots, sliced into discs

¼ teaspoon salt

1 tablespoon light brown sugar

1 teaspoon finely grated orange zest

¼ cup roasted pistachios, roughly chopped

1 Place margarine and ⅓ cup water in a sauce pot over medium-high heat.

2 Once margarine and water is boiling, add carrots and salt. Reduce heat to medium-low, cover, and simmer 12-15 minutes, or until carrots are crisp-tender.

3 Uncover pot and add the brown sugar and orange zest. Stir to combine, and then continue stirring for 5 minutes, or until most of the liquid has evaporated.

4 Stir in the chopped pistachios and serve immediately.

DR. SIEGAL'S TIPS

Pre-shelled pistachios are more readily available in grocery stores than they used to be, but you can also substitute chopped pecans or walnuts if you prefer. The good thing about those substitutions is that they are usually available in very small bags in the baking aisle of grocery stores for very little money.

CALORIES	FAT	PROTEIN	CARBS	FIBER
70	3.5g	2g	9g	4.5g

EGGPLANT AND ONION SAUTÉ

PREP TIME: 15 MINS   COOK TIME: 13 MINS   SERVES: 4

Eggplant is one of my favorite vegetables, as it is extremely low in calories, high in fiber, and a great "sponge" that absorbs any flavors you pair it with. This recipe pairs eggplant with caramelized onions, garlic, and soy sauce for a sweet and tangy Asian stir fry you can serve alongside any recipe, Asian or otherwise.

SHOPPING LIST

1 tablespoon olive oil

1 yellow onion, thinly sliced

1 medium eggplant, cut into 1-inch cubes

1 teaspoon minced garlic

1 tablespoon low-sodium soy sauce

⅛ teaspoon black pepper

1 Place olive oil and onions in a large skillet over medium-high heat and cook 3 minutes, just until onions begin to cook down.

2 Add eggplant, garlic, soy sauce, and pepper to the skillet, and sauté until eggplant is tender and onions are caramelized, about 10 minutes. Serve immediately.

DR. SIEGAL'S TIPS

You can also make this with a more Italian flavor by substituting ¼ teaspoon of salt in place of the soy sauce and adding 1 tablespoon of fresh chopped oregano.

100 calories

COLESLAW

PREP TIME: 10 MINS   CHILL TIME: 1 HOUR   SERVES: 4

Coleslaw is so much easier to make these days, now that they sell bags of pre-shredded cabbage "cole slaw mix" in the grocery stores! My coleslaw dressing recipe is creamy, but still low-fat and a whole lot of tangy. My secret ingredients—celery salt, onion powder, and ground mustard—add subtle but interesting flavors. This recipe makes 4 HUGE portions and still comes in at under 100 calories each.

100 calories

SHOPPING LIST

2 tablespoons cider vinegar

¼ cup low-fat mayonnaise

3 tablespoons low-fat milk

2 teaspoons sugar

½ teaspoon celery salt

¼ teaspoon onion powder

¼ teaspoon ground mustard

⅛ teaspoon black pepper

1 bag (16 ounces) shredded coleslaw cabbage

1 In a large bowl, whisk together all ingredients, except shredded cabbage, until well combined.

2 Add shredded cabbage to the whisked dressing in the bowl and stir all to combine.

3 Cover and refrigerate for at least 1 hour before serving.

DR. SIEGAL'S TIPS

Though the coleslaw may seem thick at first, some of the water in the cabbage will be pulled out and into the dressing as it refrigerates. The longer the refrigeration, the more watery the dressing will be (which I happen to like).

CALORIES	FAT	PROTEIN	CARBS	FIBER
90	5g	5g	8g	4g

ZESTY LEMON BROCCOLI

PREP TIME: 10 MINS   COOK TIME: 5 MINS   SERVES: 4

Lemon and broccoli are a wonderful combination on their own—but the real secret of this recipe is the Montreal steak seasoning! The seasoning (easily found in any spice aisle) packs a great mix of zesty flavors that works great on far more than just steak.

SHOPPING LIST

1 bunch broccoli, cut into florets

2 tablespoons light (and trans-fat free) margarine

1 ½ teaspoons lemon zest

½ teaspoon Montreal steak seasoning

⅛ teaspoon garlic powder

1 Add broccoli to a large pot of boiling water over high heat.

2 Boil broccoli for 5-6 minutes, or until tender.

3 Drain and return the broccoli florets to the pot. Reduce the heat to low and add all remaining ingredients, tossing just until the margarine has melted.

4 Remove from heat and serve immediately.

DR. SIEGAL'S TIPS

You can also steam the broccoli in this recipe in place of boiling it in step 2.

This recipe also works great with 1 pound of fresh sugar snap peas. Simply reduce the boiling time to 2-3 minutes.

Once you've cut the florets from the large stem of broccoli, the stem can be thinly sliced and added to a salad for a nice crunch and extra nutrition!

100 calories

CALORIES	FAT	PROTEIN	CARBS	FIBER
105	5g	8g	8g	0g

RICOTTA AND FRESH BERRY PARFAITS

PREP TIME: 15 MINS   CHILL TIME: 30 MINS   SERVES: 4

Parfaits like this are a really great low-calorie dessert, bursting with bright and colorful fresh fruit. Italian ricotta cheese is a lot like a very fine grained cottage cheese that is naturally lower in fat than you would expect from something called "cheese". I make these with part skim ricotta cheese, which is even lower in fat with very little difference in flavor.

SHOPPING LIST

1 cup part skim ricotta cheese

¼ cup low-fat milk

1 tablespoon vanilla flavored sugar-free instant pudding mix

½ cup fresh berries (strawberries, blueberries, blackberries, and/or raspberries)

mint leaves, for garnish

1 In a large bowl, combine ricotta cheese, milk, and instant pudding mix. For best results, use a hand mixer, beating until smooth and fluffy.

2 Refrigerate for 30 minutes before spooning an equal amount of the mixture into four small glasses or bowls.

3 Top each parfait with ¼ of the fresh berries. If using strawberries, slice thinly for easier eating. Garnish with a sprig of fresh mint.

DR. SIEGAL'S TIPS

Assembling these in martini or wine glasses is a real nice touch.

A really great variation on this is to add ⅛ teaspoon of ground cinnamon to the ricotta mixture in step 1 and serve topped with (only) fresh blueberries—for whatever reason, blueberries and cinnamon are a winning combination.

100 calories

CALORIES	FAT	PROTEIN	CARBS	FIBER
130	3g	7.5g	20g	1g

CHOCOLATE COVERED BANANA MOUSSE

PREP TIME: 5 MINS   CHILL TIME: 1 HOUR   SERVES: 4

This extra creamy chocolate and banana mousse has a very big secret… it's entirely dairy-free! By substituting silken tofu in place of the traditional heavy cream, you not only reduce the fat by a drastic amount, you also add more protein! Just don't tell your guests what the secret ingredient is; what they don't know will only help them!

SHOPPING LIST

1 (13 ½-ounce) package silken tofu

1 small banana, peeled

½ cup light chocolate syrup

½ teaspoon vanilla extract

1 Place all ingredients in a food processor or strong blender and secure top.

2 Blend at least 1 minute, until completely smooth.

3 Pour into 4 serving bowls or glasses and refrigerate for at least 1 hour before serving. Serve drizzled with a small amount of additional chocolate syrup.

DR. SIEGAL'S TIPS

This can be made with even fewer calories by substituting sugar-free chocolate syrup for the light chocolate syrup. You should be careful about your intake of sugar-free products though; they most likely contain "sugar alcohols" that can upset your stomach in large amounts.

100 calories

CALORIES	FAT	PROTEIN	CARBS	FIBER
95	2g	4g	16g	3.5g

STRAWBERRY MILKSHAKE

PREP TIME: 5 MINS   COOK TIME: 0 MINS   SERVES: 1

This little recipe is a two-ingredient wonder! Who needs ice cream in their milkshake when frozen strawberries do a perfectly good job of thickening the drink all on their own? With vanilla soymilk adding all the creaminess you need, you get a nice boost of protein in a light and refreshing dessert that just so happens to be dairy-free. I almost feel guilty calling it a recipe, but I definitely don't feel guilty calling it good!

SHOPPING LIST

1 cup frozen strawberries

½ cup vanilla soymilk

1 Place strawberries and soymilk in a blender and secure top.

2 Blend at least 1 minute, until completely smooth.

3 Pour into a glass and serve. That was easy! Garnish with a fresh strawberry or slice of fresh banana if desired.

DR. SIEGAL'S TIPS

Depending on the brand of frozen strawberries, you may want to add ½ packet of artificial sweetener or just a pinch of real sugar to this. Just be sure to taste it first as there is already sugar in the soymilk, and a particularly sweet batch of strawberries is all you really need.

I prefer Silk brand soymilk, as it has a very smooth and creamy taste.

100 calories

CALORIES	FAT	PROTEIN	CARBS	FIBER
130	1g	42g	19g	1g

CHEESECAKE CUPS

PREP TIME: 15 MINS   COOK TIME: 25 MINS   SERVES: 4

When you think about low-calorie eating, cheesecake may be the last thing that comes to mind—but this recipe is definitely reason to think otherwise! Without the fat of egg yolks or regular cream cheese, my secret to keeping the rich cheesecake flavor intact is actually a spoonful of cheesecake flavored instant pudding mix! Serving with mashed raspberries is an absolute must. If they aren't in season, thawing frozen raspberries before mashing will do just fine.

100 calories

SHOPPING LIST

8 ounces fat-free cream cheese

2 egg whites

3 tablespoons sugar

2 teaspoons cheesecake flavored sugar-free instant pudding mix (may use vanilla)

¼ teaspoon vanilla extract

nonstick cooking spray

1 reduced-fat graham cracker (all 4 squares), crumbled

⅓ cup fresh raspberries

1 Place oven rack in center position and preheat to 350 degrees F.

2 In a large bowl, combine cream cheese, egg whites, sugar, instant pudding mix, and vanilla extract. For best results, use a hand mixer, beating until smooth and creamy.

3 Spray 4 (4-ounce) ramekins or soufflé dishes with nonstick cooking spray, and spoon an equal amount of the cheesecake batter into each.

4 Fill a large baking dish with ½ inch of water to create a water bath. Place the filled ramekins into the water bath and bake 20-25 minutes, or until the cheesecake tops begin to crack.

5 Remove from oven and let cool before refrigerating for at least 1 hour. Use a butter knife to release from ramekins, and then completely cover the suraface with graham cracker crumbs.

6 Mash raspberries with a heavy spoon (or in a food processor) and use to dot the plate before serving.

DR. SIEGAL'S TIPS

These can be made with even fewer calories by substituting a heat stable no-calorie sweetener (such as Splenda) in place of the sugar.

CALORIES	FAT	PROTEIN	CARBS	FIBER
110	5g	1g	18g	2g

CHOCOLATE COVERED BANANA POPS

PREP TIME: 20 MINS   FREEZE TIME: 2 HRS   SERVES: 6

This is one of those recipes that we can all remember eating when we were younger! Chocolate covered bananas are not only one of the most delicious treats around but also one of the easiest to make. Personally, I love to roll them in a coating of shredded coconut and orange zest for a little bit of a tropical twist that goes perfectly with the banana.

SHOPPING LIST

2 large bananas

6 popsicle sticks

wax paper

3 tablespoons shredded coconut

1 teaspoon finely grated orange zest

½ cup semi-sweet chocolate chips

1 Peel bananas and cut each crosswise into 3 pieces. Stick a popsicle stick into the bottom of each piece.

2 Line a large plate with a piece of wax paper. Place coconut and orange zest on another, smaller plate, and toss to combine.

3 Place chocolate into a wide, shallow bowl and microwave 30 seconds. Stir, and then microwave in 15 second intervals until completely melted.

4 Dip each banana into the melted chocolate, rolling until completely coated. Then, roll each chocolate covered banana in the mixture of coconut and orange zest, just until lightly coated.

5 Place the finished banana pops on the wax paper-lined plate and freeze for at least 2 hours before serving.

DR. SIEGAL'S TIPS

The chocolate will most likely cool down as you are working, so you may need to reheat it for another 15 seconds in the middle of preparing the pops.

The coconut and orange zest mixture is optional, but highly recommended!

100 calories

200 calories

CALORIES	FAT	PROTEIN	CARBS	FIBER
225	9.5g	13g	26g	3g

TURKEY AND APRICOT STACKS

PREP TIME: 15 MINS   COOK TIME: 0 MINS   SERVES: 2

I have always been a big fan of finger foods like these interesting cracker stacks. There's just something about the combination of turkey, apricot preserves, pistachios, and creamy Babybel cheese that makes for a simple but elegant starter. With a generous serving of 6 pieces at only 225 calories, you'd be hard pressed to find a more generous party food. Just be sure to double or triple the recipe if preparing for a crowd!

SHOPPING LIST

12 reduced-fat wheat crackers

¼ pound thinly sliced deli turkey breast

2 tablespoons sugar-free apricot preserves

12 shelled pistachios

2 mini Babybel cheese wheels

1 Arrange the 12 wheat crackers on a platter and top each with an equal amount of the deli turkey breast.

2 Top the turkey on each cracker with a small spoonful of the apricot preserves, and place 1 pistachio into the preserves.

3 Remove the wax from the Babybel cheese wheels, and slice each wheel into 6 wedges. Place 1 wedge atop each cracker. Enjoy!

DR. SIEGAL'S TIPS

This is best when you ask the meat slicer at your grocery store to "shave" the turkey breast, as the meat will be easier to fold over and will stay in place on the cracker. It may fall apart, but that is just fine; simply pile it on!

The nutritional information for this recipe was tabulated with regular Babybel cheese, as it is easier to find, but they also make a "light" version of their cheese wheels that can cut each serving's calories by 20 and fat by 3g.

200 calories

CALORIES	FAT	PROTEIN	CARBS	FIBER
185	5.5g	25g	11g	1g

Hawaiian Chicken Kabobs

PREP TIME: 20 MINS   COOK TIME: 12 MINS   SERVES: 4

Chicken kabobs are proof that people like good, honest food—because even in a party environment filled with high-calorie, high-fat foods—any kind of simple, skewered meat is always the first to go! The fact that you can have two grilled kabobs of sweet and tangy chicken with chunks of pineapple in the same amount of calories as a serving of potato chips doesn't even have to be on your mind for you to want to reach for these!

200 calories

Shopping List

1 pound boneless, skinless chicken breasts, cut into 1-inch cubes

2 tablespoons low-sodium soy sauce

1 tablespoon canola oil

1 teaspoon light brown sugar

2 teaspoons minced garlic

1 tablespoon finely minced red onion

⅛ teaspoon ground ginger

1 (14-ounce) can pineapple chunks in 100% juice, drained

metal or bamboo skewers

1 Add chicken breast cubes, soy sauce, canola oil, brown sugar, garlic, red onion, and ground ginger to a food storage bag and toss all to combine. Refrigerate for 1 hour to marinate.

2 Preheat a grill, indoor grill, or grill pan to medium-high.

3 Remove chicken from marinade and thread onto skewers with the pineapple chunks, alternating between the two as you fill the skewer.

4 Place all skewers on a sheet pan and pour remaining marinade over top for one final coat.

5 Remove skewers from sheet pan and place on grill. Grill 10-12 minutes, flipping halfway through. Cut into the thickest chunk of chicken to test for doneness before serving.

Dr. Siegal's Tips

If using bamboo skewers, be sure to soak them in water for at least 30 minutes before assembling the kabobs, as they could overly char or even catch on fire if placed on the grill dry.

CALORIES	FAT	PROTEIN	CARBS	FIBER
170	5g	17g	8.5g	0g

BAKED CRAB CAKES

PREP TIME: 15 MINS   COOK TIME: 20 MINS   SERVES: 4

Ordinary crab cakes are a delicious, high-protein appetizer with only 1 major problem… they are typically sautéed in a heavy amount of oil. My recipe has all of the classic flavors of this restaurant favorite, but bakes them instead of sautéing them, cutting as much as 20 grams of fat. Makes 8 large crab cakes; 2 for each serving.

SHOPPING LIST

nonstick cooking spray

1 pound lump blue crab meat

2 large egg whites

¼ cup breadcrumbs

2 tablespoons light mayonnaise

1 tablespoon light (and trans-fat free) margarine, melted

2 tablespoons finely diced red bell pepper

1 ½ teaspoons Old Bay seasoning

1 teaspoon Worcestershire sauce

1 teaspoon baking powder

2 teaspoons parsley flakes

¼ teaspoon ground mustard

⅛ teaspoon pepper

lemon wedges, for garnish

1 Preheat oven to 375 degrees F. Spray a sheet pan with nonstick cooking spray.

2 In a large mixing bowl, carefully fold together all ingredients, except lemon wedges. For the best texture, fold the crab into the mixture last.

3 Use your hands to form the crab mixture into 8 large cakes, and place on the greased sheet pan.

4 Bake 8 minutes, flip, and then bake an additional 8-12 minutes, or until crab cakes are golden brown. Serve hot, garnished with fresh lemon wedges to squeeze over top.

DR. SIEGAL'S TIPS

Canned crab meat is nearly as good as fresh. Just be sure that the crab meat is well drained before forming the cakes.

200 calories

CALORIES	FAT	PROTEIN	CARBS	FIBER
215	3.5g	28g	18g	1g

BUFFALO CHICKEN STRIPS

PREP TIME: 20 MINS   COOK TIME: 20 MINS   SERVES: 4

Buffalo wings are an American favorite, but they are typically smothered in wing sauce that is actually only 50% hot sauce—the other 50% being high-fat butter. My recipe uses lower calorie chicken breasts cut into strips that are then breaded with the hot sauce so that it bakes right in.

200 calories

SHOPPING LIST

nonstick cooking spray

1 pound boneless, skinless chicken breasts

2 large egg whites

1 tablespoon light (and trans-fat free) margarine, melted

2 tablespoons Louisiana hot sauce

¾ cup all-purpose flour

¼ cup cornmeal

¼ teaspoon salt

¼ teaspoon pepper

1 Preheat oven to 400 degrees F. Spray a sheet pan with nonstick cooking spray.

2 Slice chicken breasts into ½ inch wide strips.

3 In a mixing bowl, whisk together egg whites, margarine, and hot sauce. In a separate bowl, combine flour, cornmeal, salt, and pepper.

4 Double bread each chicken strip by first dipping into the egg mixture, then the flour mixture, and repeating. Place onto the greased sheet pan as you go, arranging all strips in a single layer.

5 Bake 10 minutes, flip, and then bake an additional 8-10 minutes, or until breading is somewhat crispy and chicken is fully cooked throughout.

DR. SIEGAL'S TIPS

For the true Buffalo Wing experience, serve alongside celery sticks and my recipe for Blue Cheese Dressing, featured in my Wedge Salad recipe on page: 25.

CALORIES	FAT	PROTEIN	CARBS	FIBER
235	3.5g	35g	16g	1.5g

COCONUT SHRIMP

PREP TIME: 20 MINS   COOK TIME: 10 MINS   SERVES: 4

Coconut makes the perfect baked breading for these shrimp, as it browns quite nicely, even without frying. These make a great party food or appetizer, but I also suggest that you try substituting them for the spiced shrimp in my Caribbean Shrimp Salad, recipe page: 163.

SHOPPING LIST

nonstick cooking spray
1 ½ pounds large shrimp
2 large egg whites
¾ cup all-purpose flour
½ cup shredded coconut
¼ teaspoon salt
¼ teaspoon pepper

1 Preheat oven to 500 degrees F. Spray a sheet pan with nonstick cooking spray.

2 In a mixing bowl, whisk egg whites. In a separate bowl, combine flour, coconut, salt, and pepper.

3 Bread each shrimp by dipping in the egg whites and then placing in the bowl of flour and coconut. Toss shrimp in the bowl to coat, and then carefully place onto the greased sheet pan. Arrange all breaded shrimp in a single layer. Spray the tops of the shrimp with a light coating of nonstick cooking spray.

4 Bake 5 minutes, flip, and then bake an additional 5-6 minutes, or until golden brown.

DR. SIEGAL'S TIPS

Make a creamy (and spicy) apricot dipping sauce by whisking ½ cup of sugar-free apricot preserves with 1 tablespoon of low-fat mayonnaise, 1 tablespoon low-fat milk, 2 teaspoons of lime juice, and ¼ teaspoon of crushed red pepper flakes.

200 calories

Sweet Potato Home Fries
recipe page: 74

EGG WHITES BENEDICT

PREP TIME: 10 MINS   COOK TIME: 10 MINS   SERVES: 2

Eggs Benedict with Hollandaise sauce is a classic recipe that pretty much everybody loves. However, few know exactly what real Hollandaise sauce is... pure egg yolks and butter! Thankfully, Hollandaise owes a lot of its flavor to lemon juice, which I add to fat-free mayonnaise to create this healthier version with all of the spirit of the original. Each serving of this recipe includes 2 open faced Benedicts with ½ of the full sauce recipe.

SHOPPING LIST

nonstick cooking spray
4 large egg whites, beaten
2 "light" multi-grain English muffins, split and toasted
4 slices Canadian bacon
fresh parsley, for garnish

HOLLANDAISE

2 teaspoons light (and trans-fat free) margarine
¼ cup fat-free mayonnaise
1 teaspoon lemon juice
1 tablespoon Dijon mustard
2 tablespoons fat-free sour cream
1 pinch white pepper

1 Spray a small nonstick skillet with nonstick cooking spray and place over medium heat.

2 Add egg whites to the pan, cover, and let cook until no longer runny. Use a spatula to cut the eggs in half vertically and then horizontally, creating 4 separate pieces.

3 Place 2 toasted English muffin halves on each of 2 serving plates. Top all 4 halves with a slice of Canadian bacon, and then place the cooked egg pieces over that while still hot.

4 Top with warm Hollandaise sauce and garnish with fresh parsley before serving.

LOW-FAT HOLLANDAISE

Melt the margarine in a small sauce pot over medium heat. Add all remaining ingredients, stirring to combine. Once hot, immediately remove from heat and serve over the finished dish. If sauce breaks, whisk to bring it back together.

200 calories

Ham and Cream Cheese Pinwheels

PREP TIME: 15 MINS   CHILL TIME: 30 MINS   SERVES: 3

Pinwheels, or thinly sliced wraps of deli meats and cream cheese, are always a sure thing at parties. Each of the two wraps in this recipe should yield at least 10 pinwheels, making for a serving size of about 7 pinwheels, with fewer than 200 calories and only 4 grams of fat per serving.

Shopping List

4 ounces fat-free cream cheese, softened

1 tablespoon Miracle Whip Light

1 green onion (scallion), finely chopped

⅛ teaspoon garlic powder

2 whole wheat tortillas

¼ pound thin sliced deli ham

1 In a mixing bowl, combine softened cream cheese, Miracle Whip, green onion, and garlic powder to make a spread.

2 Lay the tortillas out and spread ½ of the cream cheese spread across the entire surface of each, stopping about ¾ of an inch from the edges.

3 Top the cheese spread with an equal amount of the deli ham, again covering the entire surface.

4 Roll each tortilla up as tight as possible, cover, and refrigerate for 30 minutes.

5 Using a sharp knife, cut the chilled rolls into ⅓ inch thick pinwheels. Arrange on a platter and serve.

Dr. Siegal's Tips

These can also be made with turkey or even a combination of ham and turkey. Substituting 1 tablespoon of diced roasted red pepper in place of the green onion goes particularly well with turkey pinwheels.

200 calories

CALORIES	FAT	PROTEIN	CARBS	FIBER
195	5g	10.5g	30g	7.5g

TANGY BLACK-EYED PEA SALAD

PREP TIME: 15 MINS   CHILL TIME: 1 HOUR   SERVES: 4

This chilled black-eyed pea salad is full of fresh Mexican flavors with a nice tartness coming from lemon juice. This recipe makes 4 large servings, but could easily serve 8 as a picnic side. (Nutritional information has been compiled with 4 servings in mind.) Make a full meal that comes in at only 455 calories by serving alongside my Island Spiced Tilapia with Fresh Mango, recipe page: 119.

SHOPPING LIST

2 (15-ounce) cans black-eyed peas

½ cup diced red onion

¼ cup diced yellow bell pepper

2 tomatoes, diced

1 tablespoon olive oil

juice of ½ lemon

2 tablespoons fresh chopped cilantro

1 teaspoon minced garlic

½ teaspoon salt

¼ teaspoon pepper

1 Drain and rinse black-eyed peas.

2 In a large bowl, combine all ingredients, tossing until seasonings are fully incorporated.

3 Cover and refrigerate for at least 1 hour before serving.

DR. SIEGAL'S TIPS

If you like spicier foods, I would highly suggest adding a seeded and diced jalapeño pepper to this salad.

You can also make this into more of an Italian black-eyed pea salad by substituting 1 cup of fat-free Italian salad dressing and 2 tablespoons of chopped parsley for the last 6 ingredients in the shopping list.

200 calories

CALORIES	FAT	PROTEIN	CARBS	FIBER
180	3g	11g	29g	10g

MINESTRONE SOUP

PREP TIME: 15 MINS   COOK TIME: 40 MINS   SERVES: 5

Many people think that the key to a good and rich minestrone soup is the tomato in the broth, but I've always found that the real secret is starting with a fresh chopped carrot! The flavors of the carrot, released when sautéing, combine with the tomato to give the broth that signature richness!

SHOPPING LIST

2 teaspoons olive oil

½ yellow onion, diced

1 stalk celery, sliced

1 carrot, finely chopped

1 can (14 ½ ounces) diced tomatoes

1 can (15 ½ ounces) kidney beans, drained

4 cups beef broth

2 tablespoons tomato paste

1 teaspoon Italian seasoning

¼ teaspoon garlic powder

¾ cup frozen green beans

1 cup cooked whole wheat pasta (any shape)

1 tablespoon grated Parmesan cheese

salt and pepper to taste

1 Add olive oil, onion, celery, and carrot to a large pot over medium-high heat and sauté until vegetables are soft.

2 Add diced tomatoes, kidney beans, beef broth, tomato paste, Italian seasoning, and garlic powder, and stir until combined. Bring up to a simmer and then reduce heat to medium-low. Let simmer for 30 minutes.

3 Add green beans, cooked pasta, and Parmesan cheese, and let simmer an additional 10 minutes.

4 Season with salt and pepper to taste before serving. Serve garnished with fresh parsley, if desired.

DR. SIEGAL'S TIPS

Be sure to wait until the soup is done cooking before adding salt, as the soup will reduce as it simmers, making the remaining liquid saltier. You may not even need any additional salt, but I definitely suggest adding some fresh ground black pepper.

200 calories

CALORIES	FAT	PROTEIN	CARBS	FIBER
180	9g	16g	4g	2g

ITALIAN WEDDING SOUP

PREP TIME: 20 MINS   COOK TIME: 22 MINS   SERVES: 4

My version of Italian Wedding Soup has all of the flavors of homemade without all of the added calories. I use lean ground turkey to form the small meatballs and skip the traditional pearls of pasta (which never really adds enough texture for their caloric value) in favor of diced fresh tomato.

200 calories

SHOPPING LIST

½ pound lean ground turkey
¼ teaspoon ground sage
¼ teaspoon Italian seasoning
¼ teaspoon salt
¼ teaspoon pepper
1 tablespoon olive oil
4 cups chicken broth
1 tomato, diced
1 teaspoon onion powder
¾ teaspoon garlic powder
1 (10-ounce) bag frozen chopped spinach
salt and pepper to taste
4 tablespoons shredded Parmesan cheese

1 In a large bowl, combine ground turkey, sage, Italian seasoning, salt, and pepper to create the meatball mix. Form into tiny meatballs about ½ inch tall with your fingers or a melon baller.

2 Place olive oil in a large nonstick skillet over medium-high heat. Add meatballs and brown on all sides, about 8 minutes.

3 Meanwhile, add chicken broth to a large pot over high heat. Bring up to a simmer and then reduce heat to medium-low.

4 Add the browned meatballs, diced tomato, onion powder, and garlic powder to the chicken broth, and let simmer 10 minutes.

5 Add the chopped spinach and let simmer an additional 4 minutes before adding salt and pepper to taste. Serve each bowl topped with 1 tablespoon of the shredded Parmesan cheese.

DR. SIEGAL'S TIPS

You can also make the meatballs out of Italian flavored ground turkey and skip adding all of the seasonings in step 1. I have seen Italian flavored ground turkey next to the regular ground turkey in some grocery stores.

CALORIES	FAT	PROTEIN	CARBS	FIBER
170	11g	7.5g	12g	2.5g

GREEK SALAD

PREP TIME: 20 MINS   CHILL TIME: 30 MINS   SERVES: 4

This Greek Salad with a creamy Greek dressing is so big and satisfying that it is almost an entire meal wrapped up in only 170 calories. Though it isn't exactly traditional, I love the tang of pickled banana pepper rings in my Greek Salad. Add 6 ounces of cooked chicken for a meal that is only 335 calories.

SHOPPING LIST

1 (10-ounce) bag romaine lettuce blend

1 small cucumber, sliced

1 large tomato, halved and sliced

½ small red onion, thinly sliced

¼ cup jarred banana pepper rings

½ cup Kalamata olives

¾ cup crumbled feta cheese

GREEK DRESSING

½ cup plain yogurt

1 tablespoon olive oil

1 tablespoon lemon juice

1 teaspoon minced garlic

¾ teaspoon dry oregano

salt and pepper

1 Split the romaine lettuce equally between 4 bowls.

2 Top the lettuce in each bowl with a few slices of cucumber, tomato, and red onion. Sprinkle banana pepper rings and Kalamata olives around the circumference of each salad.

3 Place a small mound of the feta cheese in the center of each salad.

4 Serve salads drizzled with the Greek Dressing.

GREEK DRESSING

In a small bowl, whisk together all ingredients. Add salt and pepper to taste, and chill 30 minutes to let the flavors combine.

200 calories

CALORIES	FAT	PROTEIN	CARBS	FIBER
175	8g	6g	22g	4.5g

MANDARIN ORANGE SALAD

PREP TIME: 20 MINS   CHILL TIME: 1 HOUR   SERVES: 4

This Asian salad is loaded with fresh and crisp romaine lettuce, carrots, and raw snap peas. Mandarin oranges keep things interesting while roasted peanuts add the crunch that you would normally get from high carbohydrate noodles or croutons. Just be sure to choose a can of Mandarin oranges that says that it is packed in fruit juice, not sugary syrup, as the added calories are unnecessary.

SHOPPING LIST

1 (10-ounce) bag romaine lettuce blend

½ cup shredded carrots

1 cup snap peas

4 green onions, sliced

1 (11-ounce) can mandarin oranges, drained

¼ cup roasted peanuts

ASIAN DRESSING

⅓ cup water

1 tablespoon sesame oil

1 tablespoon cider vinegar

1 tablespoon soy sauce

½ teaspoon minced garlic

3 teaspoons light brown sugar

½ teaspoon cornstarch

1 Split the romaine lettuce equally between 4 bowls.

2 Top the lettuce in each bowl with an equal amount of the shredded carrots, snap peas, and green onions.

3 Place a small mound of the mandarin oranges in the center of each salad.

4 Sprinkle peanuts around the circumference of each salad and serve drizzled with Asian dressing.

ASIAN DRESSING

Whisk together all ingredients in a small sauce pan over medium-high heat. Bring up to a boil, reduce heat to medium-low, and let simmer for 2 minutes, or until slightly thickened. Refrigerate for at least 1 hour, or until chilled.

200 calories

CALORIES	FAT	PROTEIN	CARBS	FIBER
215	5g	22g	22g	1g

NEW ENGLAND CLAM CHOWDER

PREP TIME: 15 MINS   COOK TIME: 17 MINS   SERVES: 4

New England Clam Chowder, like most classic dishes, is typically rich and extremely high in fat. No one was paying attention to fat grams when these dishes were invented, but that doesn't mean they can't be reinvented in a way that tastes great! In fact, I think you'd have a pretty hard time telling a bowl of this apart from any you'd get at a sit-down restaurant in New England.

SHOPPING LIST

3 slices turkey bacon, chopped

1 tablespoon light (and trans-fat free) margarine

1 stalk celery, chopped

1 small onion, chopped

½ cup diced new potatoes

2 (10-ounce) cans chopped or minced baby clams, with juice

2 cups low-fat milk

1 bay leaf

⅛ teaspoon garlic powder

½ teaspoon dry thyme

½ cup fat-free half and half

¼ cup all-purpose flour

salt and pepper to taste

1 Add chopped bacon, margarine, celery, and onion to a large pot over medium-high heat and sauté until vegetables are soft, about 5 minutes.

2 Add potatoes to the pot and sauté an additional 2 minutes.

3 Add clams with juice, milk, bay leaf, garlic powder, and thyme to the pot and stir until combined. Bring up to a simmer and then reduce heat to medium-low. Cover and let simmer 5 minutes.

4 In a mixing bowl, whisk together half and half and flour. Slowly add this mixture into the simmering pot, stirring until soup is thickened. Let the thickened soup continue simmering for 4-5 minutes, or until potatoes are nice and tender. Add salt and pepper to taste and serve immediately.

DR. SIEGAL'S TIPS

Canned clams typically have plenty of salt in the broth, so you may not even need any additional salt; though, I definitely suggest adding some fresh ground black pepper.

CALORIES	FAT	PROTEIN	CARBS	FIBER
170	9.5g	7.5g	15g	2g

CAESAR SALAD WITH WHOLE WHEAT CROUTONS

PREP TIME: 25 MINS   COOK TIME: 22 MINS   SERVES: 4

While this recipe is about as classic as it gets, the lower-calorie preparation definitely isn't! With homemade croutons made from whole wheat bread and a very creamy dressing made with plain yogurt, this recipe is not only lower in calories than the traditional version, but the calories are coming from much healthier sources.

SHOPPING LIST

1 (10-ounce) bag romaine lettuce blend
¼ cup shredded Parmesan cheese

CAESAR DRESSING

½ cup plain yogurt
¼ cup fat-free mayonnaise
2 tablespoons grated Parmesan cheese
1 teaspoon minced garlic
½ teaspoon Worcestershire sauce
⅛ teaspoon salt
⅛ teaspoon pepper

WHOLE WHEAT CROUTONS

2 slices whole wheat bread
1 tablespoon light (and trans-fat free) margarine, melted
⅛ teaspoon garlic powder
salt and pepper

1 In a large bowl, toss romaine lettuce in the Caesar dressing.

2 Split the dressed lettuce equally between 4 serving bowls.

3 Top each salad with an equal amount of the whole wheat croutons and a sprinkling of shredded Parmesan cheese.

CAESAR DRESSING

In a small bowl, whisk together all dressing ingredients. Cover and refrigerate 30 minutes to let the flavors combine. For the traditional Caesar salad taste, you can add ½ teaspoon of anchovy paste.

WHOLE WHEAT CROUTONS

Preheat oven to 300 degrees. Cut each slice of whole wheat bread into 16 cubes and place into a mixing bowl. Add the melted butter and toss to coat. Spread in a single layer on a sheet pan, and then sprinkle garlic powder and a generous amount of salt and pepper over top. Bake 10 minutes, flip croutons, and then bake an additional 10-12 minutes, or until crispy.

200 calories

CALORIES	FAT	PROTEIN	CARBS	FIBER
215	7g	3.5g	36g	6g

SWEET POTATO HOME FRIES

PREP TIME: 25 MINS   COOK TIME: 12 MINS   SERVES: 4

Sweet potatoes and onions go surprisingly well together, especially when served alongside savory chicken or salmon dishes. So even though these are called "Home Fries," feel free to serve them with your favorite dinner entrée in place of a less nutritious white potato side dish. That being said, these really are the perfect side for my Tomato and Basil Omelet, recipe page: 23.

SHOPPING LIST

4 cups cubed sweet potato, about ⅓ inch thick

2 tablespoons olive oil

1 small yellow onion, diced

½ teaspoon paprika

⅛ teaspoon onion powder

½ teaspoon salt

¼ teaspoon black pepper

1 Place cubed sweet potato in a large bowl of cold water and let sit 25 minutes. Drain well and pat dry with paper towels.

2 Heat olive oil in a large skillet over medium-high heat for 1 minute.

3 Add sweet potatoes to the skillet and sauté 5 minutes.

4 Add onions, paprika, onion powder, salt, and pepper to the skillet, and continue sautéing until sweet potatoes are browned on the outside and tender on the inside and onions are cooked, about 4-6 more minutes. Serve immediately.

DR. SIEGAL'S TIPS

For a real spicy kick to go along with the sweet of the sweet potatoes, try adding a small pinch of cayenne pepper. This will turn these home fries into the perfect accompaniment to Mexican food.

200 calories

CALORIES	FAT	PROTEIN	CARBS	FIBER
160	4.5g	3g	28g	7.5g

CARROT AND TURNIP MASH

PREP TIME: 20 MINS   COOK TIME: 15 MINS   SERVES: 4

This is a great holiday (or any day) dish that gives you all the benefits of vegetables with all of the texture of a starchy side. Serve underneath my Maple Glazed Salmon, recipe page: 153, for a complete and very hearty meal with only 560 calories. This recipe makes 4 gigantic servings but could definitely serve as many as 8 during the holidays when other side dishes would be on the table.

SHOPPING LIST

2 pounds carrots

2 turnips

3 tablespoons light (and trans-fat free) margarine

2 tablespoons low-fat milk

1 tablespoon light brown sugar

¼ teaspoon salt

⅛ teaspoon pepper

1 pinch nutmeg

1 Peel carrots and turnips. Slice carrots into discs and chop turnips into small chunks.

2 Place carrots and turnips in a pot of boiling water, cover, and boil 15 minutes, or until carrots are very tender. Drain well.

3 Return the drained vegetables to the pot and cover with remaining ingredients. Use a potato masher to mash well. (Turnips will mash less smoothly than carrots.) Serve immediately.

DR. SIEGAL'S TIPS

If the mixture cools before you've completely mashed it, simply turn the stove on low and stir well, just until the mash has come back up to temperature.

You can also use 1 large rutabaga in place of the turnips if you prefer or if it is all that you can find at your local grocery store.

200 calories

CALORIES	FAT	PROTEIN	CARBS	FIBER
225	8g	10g	32g	7g

Mediterranean Penne Pasta

PREP TIME: 15 MINS   COOK TIME: 20 MINS   SERVES: 6

Whole wheat pasta can supply a very good amount of dietary fiber, which will help you feel fuller longer—quite the opposite effect of regular, white pasta. The simple, fresh ingredients tossed with the pasta in this recipe are classic flavors of the Mediterranean. Whether this recipe is more Greek or Italian—I can't say—but I do know that it's one satisfying side dish!

Shopping List

8 ounces whole wheat penne pasta

1 tablespoon olive oil

1 tomato, diced

8 ounces marinated artichoke hearts, drained

1 can (2.25 ounces) sliced black olives

2 teaspoons minced garlic

¼ teaspoon dry oregano

¼ teaspoon salt

⅛ teaspoon pepper

½ cup reduced-fat feta cheese

fresh chopped parsley, for garnish

1 Boil pasta according to the directions on the box. Reserve ½ cup of the pasta boiling water before straining pasta.

2 Transfer strained pasta to a large nonstick skillet over medium heat (do not rinse pasta!).

3 Add the reserved ½ cup pasta boiling water, olive oil, diced tomato, artichoke hearts, black olives, minced garlic, oregano, salt, and pepper to the skillet, and toss all to combine.

4 Bring up to a simmer and let cook 4-5 minutes, stirring constantly, just until liquid begins to thicken.

5 Stir in feta cheese and chopped parsley just before serving.

Dr. Siegal's Tips

You can skip the dry oregano and substitute fresh chopped oregano in place of the parsley in step 5 for even fresher flavors. About 1 tablespoon of chopped fresh oregano works great.

I always use jarred garlic when I cook as fresh can be very, very overwhelming. I'd recommend using only 1 clove of fresh garlic if you decide to go that route.

200 calories

CALORIES	FAT	PROTEIN	CARBS	FIBER
225	6g	6g	39g	2.5g

BROWN RICE AND BROCCOLI PILAF

PREP TIME: 10 MINS   COOK TIME: 55 MINS   SERVES: 4

While white and brown rice are very similar in calorie content, the difference in nutrition is much more defined. White rice is just brown rice that has been stripped of pretty much all of its fiber content and many of its vitamins in processing. Using brown rice in a pilaf like this one takes a little longer to cook, but the nutritional benefits are a no-brainer.

200 calories

SHOPPING LIST

1 tablespoon olive oil
¾ cup diced yellow onion
1 tablespoon light (and trans-fat free) margarine
2 teaspoons minced garlic
1 cup long-grain brown rice
3 ½ cups reduced-sodium chicken broth
1 teaspoon lemon juice
⅛ teaspoon poultry seasoning
¼ teaspoon celery salt
¼ teaspoon pepper
¾ cup finely chopped broccoli florets

1 Place olive oil and onion in a pot over medium-high heat and sauté until onions are soft, about 4 minutes.

2 Add margarine, garlic, and brown rice to the pot and sauté for 1 minute.

3 Add all remaining ingredients, except broccoli, and stir to combine. Bring up to a boil and then reduce heat to low. Cover and simmer for 30 minutes.

4 Stir in chopped broccoli, re-cover, and simmer an additional 20 minutes, or until rice is tender. Let sit 5 minutes before fluffing with a fork and serving.

DR. SIEGAL'S TIPS

Serve topped with grated or shaved Parmesan cheese for even more flavor. 2 teaspoons of grated Parmesan cheese will only add around 20 calories.

CALORIES	FAT	PROTEIN	CARBS	FIBER
160	8g	12g	11g	4g

CAULIFLOWER AU GRATIN

PREP TIME: 15 MINS   COOK TIME: 20 MINS   SERVES: 4

"Au gratin" is a French term for dishes topped with breadcrumbs and butter and placed under the broiler to brown. Somewhere along the line, someone started adding cheese to these dishes and the taste (and calories) went up to another level! Cauliflower Au Gratin is one of the most popular dishes cooked in this method. I have broken all of the traditional "au gratin" rules with my (much healthier) interpretation. I've skipped the breadcrumbs, the extra butter, and the broiling as I find that the cheese is where all the flavor is. It bakes up nice and crispy all on its own.

SHOPPING LIST

nonstick cooking spray
florets of 1 head cauliflower
⅔ cup low-fat milk
2 egg whites
1 tablespoon light (and trans-fat free) margarine, melted
2 tablespoons grated Parmesan cheese
¼ teaspoon salt
⅛ teaspoon pepper
1 tiny pinch nutmeg
¾ cup shredded Swiss cheese

1 Preheat oven to 400 degrees F. Spray an 8x8 baking dish with nonstick cooking spray.

2 Add cauliflower florets to a large pot of boiling water over high heat, cover, and boil 5-6 minutes, just until crisp-tender. Drain well and place in baking dish.

3 In a mixing bowl, whisk together milk, egg whites, melted margarine, Parmesan cheese, salt, pepper, and nutmeg. Pour over cauliflower in baking dish.

4 Top cauliflower and sauce with the shredded Swiss cheese and bake 10-14 minutes, until cheese begins to brown. Let cool 5 minutes before serving.

DR. SIEGAL'S TIPS

You can also prepare this exact same recipe with broccoli in place of the cauliflower; or try a combination of the two!

200 calories

CALORIES	FAT	PROTEIN	CARBS	FIBER
230	8g	10g	29g	4g

QUINOA ALMONDINE

PREP TIME: 10 MINS   COOK TIME: 20 MINS   SERVES: 4

Quinoa makes a great pilaf-style side dish, as it is very similar to a cereal grain like barley or cracked wheat, but it is not a grain at all. Available in pretty much all grocery stores these days by the wild rice or in the organic foods section, the great thing about quinoa is that it is high in amino acids that are typically only found in meat. These amino acids help keep you full and satisfied.

SHOPPING LIST

⅓ cup slivered almonds

1 tablespoon light (and trans-fat free) margarine

1 cup quinoa

2 cups chicken broth

2 teaspoons parsley flakes

⅛ teaspoon onion powder

⅛ teaspoon garlic powder

⅛ teaspoon celery salt

⅛ teaspoon pepper

1 Preheat oven to 350 degrees F. Spread slivered almonds across the bottom of a sheet pan and bake 10 minutes, just until lightly toasted. Remove from oven and set aside.

2 Meanwhile, add all remaining ingredients to a sauce pot over medium-high heat.

3 Bring quinoa mixture up to a boil, and then reduce heat to low, cover, and let simmer for 10 minutes.

4 Remove from heat and let sit 5 minutes before fluffing with a fork. Stir in toasted almonds and serve immediately.

DR. SIEGAL'S TIPS

Quinoa needs to be well rinsed before cooking, but most sold in stores these days is already pre-rinsed. The kind that I find most often in stores is by a brand called Ancient Harvest and comes in a green box. This brand is already pre-rinsed and ready to prepare.

Around the holidays, adding a handful of dried cranberries to this recipe is always a good idea. The best time to add them is in step 4, before letting the quinoa sit for 5 minutes. It's just enough time to soften the cranberries.

CALORIES	FAT	PROTEIN	CARBS	FIBER
195	7g	5g	28g	3g

COCONUT AND OAT BARS

PREP TIME: 15 MINS   COOK TIME: 20 MINS   SERVES: 6

These bars remind me of a delicious combination of granola bars and old-fashioned coconut macaroons. While this recipe could easily be cut into 12 smaller bars for a party or get-together, the nutrition facts have been tabulated for 6 larger, more realistic servings.

SHOPPING LIST

nonstick cooking spray

3 large egg whites

½ cup light brown sugar

2 tablespoons light (and trans-fat free) margarine, melted

½ teaspoon vanilla extract

¼ teaspoon baking soda

⅛ teaspoon salt

1 cup old fashioned oats

1 cup shredded coconut

⅓ cup all-purpose flour

1 Preheat oven to 350 degrees F. Spray an 8x8 baking dish with nonstick cooking spray.

2 In a large mixing bowl, whisk together egg whites, brown sugar, margarine, vanilla extract, baking soda, and salt.

3 Fold in oats, coconut, and flour until all is combined into a thick batter.

4 Spread batter into the greased baking dish. Bake for 15-20 minutes, or until bars begin to brown and the center is springy to the touch.

5 Let cool 10 minutes before slicing down the center vertically and then twice horizontally to create 6 bars.

DR. SIEGAL'S TIPS

Shredded coconut is sold in bags in the baking section. Sweetened shredded coconut will taste better, but unsweetened shredded coconut (if available at your store) will cut the calories by about 25 per serving.

200 calories

CALORIES	FAT	PROTEIN	CARBS	FIBER
180	6g	5g	27g	2g

DOUBLE CHOCOLATE MUFFINS

PREP TIME: 15 MINS   COOK TIME: 22 MINS   SERVES: 6

I am not a big fan of this recipe. It's just too good for its own good! Though these are called muffins, they are as moist and delicious as chocolate cake. With both cocoa and semi-sweet chocolate chips, these are so delicious that I had to keep the amounts down to only 6 muffins to discourage overindulging!

SHOPPING LIST

¾ cup whole wheat flour

⅓ cup light brown sugar

3 tablespoons unsweetened cocoa powder

½ teaspoon baking powder

⅛ teaspoon salt

⅓ cup fat-free sour cream

3 tablespoons low-fat milk

1 large egg

2 tablespoons light (and trans-fat free) margarine, melted

½ teaspoon vanilla extract

¼ cup semi-sweet chocolate chips

1 Preheat oven to 325 degrees F. Line a 6 cup muffin tin with paper liners or spray well with nonstick cooking spray.

2 In a large mixing bowl, combine whole wheat flour, light brown sugar, cocoa powder, baking powder, and salt.

3 In a separate mixing bowl, whisk together sour cream, milk, egg, margarine, and vanilla extract.

4 Fold the whisked wet ingredients into the combined dry ingredients until fully mixed and then gently fold in chocolate chips.

5 Drop muffin batter into the 6 muffin cups until each is no more than ¾ full. Bake for 18-22 minutes, or until a toothpick inserted into the center comes out mostly clean. Serve warm or at room temperature.

DR. SIEGAL'S TIPS

These are best when fresh out of the oven!

200 calories

CALORIES	FAT	PROTEIN	CARBS	FIBER
200	4g	4g	38g	6g

RASPBERRY PEACH COBBLER

PREP TIME: 20 MINS   COOK TIME: 30 MINS   SERVES: 6

Cobbler is one of the easiest baked goods you can make, and that isn't even the biggest reason to fall in love with this dessert all over again. The reason that I really love it is that it has all of the taste of a good fruit pie, without all of the fat that you'd find in a typical pie crust.

SHOPPING LIST

nonstick cooking spray

1 pound frozen peach slices, thawed

1 pint raspberries

¼ cup light brown sugar

1 tablespoon all-purpose flour

½ teaspoon ground cinnamon

TOPPING

¾ cup old fashioned oats

¼ cup light brown sugar

3 tablespoons all-purpose flour

3 tablespoons light (and trans-fat free) margarine, melted

½ teaspoon cinnamon

1 Preheat oven to 400 degrees F. Spray an 8x8 baking dish with nonstick cooking spray.

2 In a large mixing bowl, combine peaches, raspberries, brown sugar, flour, and cinnamon, and pour into the greased baking dish.

3 In a separate bowl, combine all Topping ingredients and drop by the large spoonful over top the fruit mixture in the baking dish.

4 Bake for 30 minutes, or until bubbly hot and the topping has begun to brown. Let cool for at least 5 minutes before spooning into serving bowls.

DR. SIEGAL'S TIPS

Try serving topped with a large spoonful of light vanilla yogurt. It will only add about 15 calories per serving.

200 calories

CALORIES	FAT	PROTEIN	CARBS	FIBER
190	6g	8g	30g	0.5g

TIRAMISU MINIS

PREP TIME: 10 MINS   CHILL TIME: 30 MINS   SERVES: 4

Tiramisu is traditionally made with tons of egg yolks and Italian mascarpone cheese, which are both extremely high in fat. My recipe uses instant pudding made with skim milk in the place of those higher fat ingredients for a lighter, but still full-flavored, dessert. My other substitutions, reduced-fat vanilla wafers in place of the traditional ladyfinger biscuits and instant coffee granules in place of the espresso, are simply easier to find at my local grocery store.

SHOPPING LIST

16 reduced-fat vanilla wafer cookies

1 ¾ cups skim milk

1 teaspoon instant coffee granules

1 box vanilla flavored sugar-free instant pudding mix

1 packet sugar-free hot cocoa mix

4 dark chocolate squares (such as Ghirardelli 60% cocoa squares)

1 Lay out 4 serving bowls or glasses.

2 Dip 3 vanilla wafers into the skim milk and place at the bottom of one of the serving bowls. Sprinkle ¼ teaspoon of instant coffee granules over the wafers at the bottom of the bowl. Repeat with the other 3 bowls. Reserve the remaining 4 vanilla wafers.

3 Whisk instant pudding mix into the remaining skim milk until smooth and free of lumps. Pour an equal amount into each serving bowl.

4 Sprinkle an equal amount of the powdered hot cocoa mix over top of the pudding in each bowl. Refrigerate for at least 30 minutes. (3-4 hours is even better!)

5 Serve each tiramisu garnished with 1 vanilla wafer and 1 square of dark chocolate.

DR. SIEGAL'S TIPS

You can use this same method to make Boston Cream Pie Minis by skipping the instant coffee granules in step 2 and substituting a drizzle of sugar-free chocolate syrup for the hot cocoa mix in step 4.

You can also prepare this in 3 layers in a slender glass, alternating between 1 vanilla wafer, ⅓ of the coffee granules, and ⅓ of the pudding mix.

200 calories

CALORIES	FAT	PROTEIN	CARBS	FIBER
160	3.5g	3g	23g	2g

BLUEBERRY ALMOND PANNA COTTA

PREP TIME: 20 MINS   CHILL TIME: 4+ HRS   SERVES: 4

Panna Cotta is a creamy Italian gelatin dessert that is typically made with high-fat heavy cream that can leave you with a dessert with nearly 25 grams of fat. I've managed to bring the fat down to only 3.5 grams per serving in my version, which is topped with a delicious blueberry sauce and toasted almonds.

200 calories

SHOPPING LIST

1 (.25-ounce) envelope unflavored gelatin
½ cup low-fat milk
2 cups fat-free half and half
½ cup bulk sugar substitute
¼ teaspoon almond extract
6 ounces blueberries
1 tablespoon light brown sugar
⅛ teaspoon cinnamon
¼ cup sliced almonds, toasted

1 Stir gelatin into the low-fat milk and let sit 5 minutes.

2 Meanwhile, place the fat-free half and half in a sauce pan over medium heat and bring up to a simmer.

3 Add gelatin and milk mixture to the simmering half and half, and then remove from heat. Add sugar substitute and almond extract, and stir constantly, until all gelatin has dissolved.

4 Pour mixture into 4 small bowls or ramekins, cover, and refrigerate for at least 4 hours, or until set.

5 Meanwhile, create the blueberry sauce by placing blueberries, brown sugar, cinnamon, and ½ cup of water in a sauce pan over medium heat. Simmer for 4-6 minutes, using a potato masher or heavy spoon to mash the blueberries as they cook. Once mixture has slightly thickened, remove from heat and refrigerate until ready to serve the Panna Cotta.

6 Use a knife around the circumference of each chilled Panna Cotta to release from their ramekins and flip onto individual serving plates. Top each with an equal amount of the blueberry sauce and a sprinkling of toasted almonds before serving.

DR. SIEGAL'S TIPS

You can toast sliced almonds by spreading them out on a sheet pan and baking in a 350 degree oven until golden brown, only 5-8 minutes.

300 calories

CALORIES	FAT	PROTEIN	CARBS	FIBER
260	9g	18g	23g	7g

HAM, SPINACH, AND WHITE BEAN SOUP

PREP TIME: 15 MINS   COOK TIME: 45 MINS   SERVES: 4

Italian cannellini beans are nice, buttery white beans that are closely related to kidney beans. Combining these beans with ham is a tried and true way to make some really great soup! Many recipes puree white beans into a soup that is similar to split pea, but I like to keep them whole and add chopped spinach to bulk up the soup instead.

SHOPPING LIST

1 tablespoon olive oil

1 small yellow onion, diced

8 ounces diced ham

1 can (15 ½ ounces) cannellini beans, drained

4 cups reduced-sodium chicken broth

1 cup water

1 tablespoon lemon juice

2 teaspoons minced garlic

2 teaspoons fresh chopped sage

1 (10-ounce) package frozen chopped spinach

salt and pepper to taste

1 Place olive oil and onion in a large pot over medium-high heat and sauté until onions begin to caramelize, about 5 minutes.

2 Add diced ham and continue sautéing for 1 minute.

3 Add all remaining ingredients, except spinach, and stir to combine. Bring up to a boil and then reduce heat to medium-low. Let simmer uncovered for 30 minutes.

4 Add frozen spinach and let simmer an additional 10 minutes. Season with salt and pepper to taste before serving. Serve garnished with a fresh sage leaf, if desired.

DR. SIEGAL'S TIPS

Freshly chopped sage is what really makes this recipe shine, but you can substitute ground sage in a pinch. Ground sage is very potent, so you should only add about ¼ of a teaspoon.

300 calories

CALORIES	FAT	PROTEIN	CARBS	FIBER
275	8g	32g	20g	4g

BEEF AND BARLEY STEW

PREP TIME: 15 MINS   COOK TIME: 1 ½ HOURS   SERVES: 6

Barley is a wonderful grain that has eight essential amino acids, so even though this stew contains only 275 calories a bowl, your body will still be quite satisfied and stay fuller longer than with other foods you could eat in the same amount of calories. Another food that is loaded with amino acids… the lean beef that also makes an appearance in this dish!

300 calories

SHOPPING LIST

1 tablespoon olive oil

1 ½ pounds lean stew meat

2 tablespoons all-purpose flour

2 stalks celery, chopped

1 small onion, chopped

¼ cup dry barley

4 cups beef broth

1 (14 ½-ounce) can diced tomatoes

2 tablespoons tomato paste

1 bay leaf

¼ teaspoon thyme

¼ teaspoon garlic powder

⅛ teaspoon pepper

1 cup frozen peas and carrots

1 cup frozen corn kernels

salt to taste

1 Add olive oil to a large pot over medium-high heat.

2 Toss stew meat in flour until all pieces are well coated. Add the coated stew meat to the pot and sauté until all pieces are beginning to brown, about 5 minutes

3 Add celery, onion, and barley to the pot and continue sautéing about 8 minutes, or until onion is translucent.

4 Add beef broth, diced tomatoes, tomato paste, bay leaf, thyme, garlic powder, and pepper, stirring until combined. Bring up to a simmer and then reduce heat to medium-low. Let simmer for 1 hour.

5 Add frozen vegetables and 1 cup of tap water, and let simmer an additional 20 minutes. Salt to taste before serving.

DR. SIEGAL'S TIPS

You can use any combination of frozen vegetables you wish in place of the peas, carrots, and corn in step 5. A traditional frozen succotash mix works really great too, especially with baby lima beans!

CALORIES	FAT	PROTEIN	CARBS	FIBER
270	6g	31g	25g	6.5g

Very Veggie Turkey Chili

PREP TIME: 20 MINS   COOK TIME: 55 MINS   SERVES: 4

This chili recipe is definitely not your ordinary bowl of winter warmth! Not only is it made with ground turkey, but it also substitutes a bounty of vegetables, like celery, zucchini, and corn, in place of the typical beans. While beans are entirely good for you, the vegetables make for something delicious and different.

Shopping List

1 tablespoon olive oil
1 pound extra lean ground turkey
1 yellow onion, chopped
3 stalks celery, chopped
1 green bell pepper, chopped
2 (15-ounce) cans diced tomatoes, with juice
1 (8-ounce) can tomato sauce
½ cup chicken broth
2 teaspoons chili powder
¼ teaspoon cumin
½ teaspoon garlic powder
1 cup diced zucchini
1 cup frozen corn kernels
salt and pepper

1 Place olive oil and ground turkey in a large pot over medium-high heat and sauté until nearly browned, about 6 minutes.

2 Add onion, celery, and bell pepper to the pot and continue sautéing until onion is translucent, about 4 minutes.

3 Add all remaining ingredients, except zucchini and corn, and bring up to a boil. Reduce heat to medium-low and let simmer 30 minutes.

4 Stir in diced zucchini and frozen corn and let simmer an additional 15 minutes. Add salt and pepper to taste and serve.

300 calories

Dr. Siegal's Tips

Extra lean ground turkey is usually labeled as "ground turkey breast" and is 98% or 99% fat free.

CALORIES	FAT	PROTEIN	CARBS	FIBER
310	7.5g	25g	39g	3g

CHICKEN AND WILD RICE SOUP

PREP TIME: 20 MINS   COOK TIME: 45 MINS   SERVES: 4

This soup is so full of chicken, rice, and vegetables that I should probably call it a stew! A great recipe to make out of leftover chicken, you can also make this with pre-cooked chicken "short cuts" sold in the grocery store. Or, if you would like to go fully homemade, simply add 2 chopped raw chicken breasts in step 1, cooking until white throughout before continuing on with the recipe.

SHOPPING LIST

1 tablespoon olive oil

1 yellow onion, diced

2 stalks celery, sliced

2 teaspoons minced garlic

1 ½ cups chopped cooked chicken

4 cups reduced-sodium chicken broth

2 cups vegetable broth

1 (6-ounce) box long grain and wild rice

2 teaspoons fresh thyme leaves

2 teaspoons parsley flakes

¼ teaspoon poultry seasoning

¼ teaspoon white pepper

1 cup frozen peas and carrots

1 Place olive oil, onion, and celery in a large pot over medium-high heat, and sauté until onions turn translucent, about 5 minutes.

2 Add garlic and chicken, and continue sautéing for 1 minute.

3 Add all remaining ingredients, except frozen peas and carrots, and stir to combine. Bring up to a boil and then reduce heat to medium-low. Let simmer, uncovered, for 30 minutes.

4 Add frozen peas and carrots, and let simmer an additional 10 minutes before serving.

DR. SIEGAL'S TIPS

I use a box of Uncle Ben's brand Long Grain and Wild Rice to make this soup, discarding the included seasoning packet.

300 calories

CALORIES	FAT	PROTEIN	CARBS	FIBER
260	12g	20g	25g	8g

INSIDE-OUT PORTABELLA SWISS BURGERS

PREP TIME: 20 MINS   COOK TIME: 10 MINS   SERVES: 2

Large portabella mushroom caps have often been used as an alternative to traditional ground beef burgers, as they have a nice meaty flavor when grilled. My recipe doubles up on the mushroom caps in a very unique way—in place of the bun! Filled with all of your favorite fixings and condiments, it's all the flavors you love in a completely new package.

SHOPPING LIST

4 large portabella mushroom caps, stems removed

1 tablespoon olive oil

½ teaspoon Montreal steak seasoning

2 slices reduced-fat Swiss cheese

4 large lettuce leaves

1 tomato, sliced

4 slices onion

your favorite condiments

1 Preheat an indoor or outdoor grill (or grill pan) to medium-high.

2 Brush portabella mushroom caps with olive oil and sprinkle both sides generously with Montreal steak seasoning.

3 Grill mushroom caps, bottom side down, for 3-5 minutes, or until grill marks are well defined. Flip caps and grill for 3 minutes on the opposite side.

4 Top 2 caps with Swiss cheese and grill all caps 2 additional minutes, until cheese begins to melt.

5 Assemble 2 Inside-Out burgers by placing 2 lettuce leaves, 2 tomato slices, 2 onion slices, and a generous amount of your favorite condiments in between a top and bottom grilled portabella "bun". Serve with a knife and fork, or plenty of napkins!

DR. SIEGAL'S TIPS

I use the cheese topped portabella as the bottom bun and place the condiments on the top portabella.

Use as much mustard as you like. I prefer the lower calories of no sugar added ketchup and relish, but the traditional versions can be used in smaller amounts.

Mayonnaise should be limited to low-fat or fat-free varieties.

300 calories

CALORIES	FAT	PROTEIN	CARBS	FIBER
340	8g	27g	37g	6g

TURKEY, CUCUMBER, AND HUMMUS WRAPS

PREP TIME: 20 MINS   COOK TIME: 0 MINS   SERVES: 2

Hummus, a creamy spread made from chickpeas, is a great alternative to loading sandwiches up with high-fat mayonnaise or cheese. While hummus isn't amazingly low in calories, it makes up for that by being high in vitamins, protein, and fiber. This recipe makes 2 full wraps—1 per serving—each stuffed with ¼ pound of turkey breast!

SHOPPING LIST

½ cucumber, peeled and diced

2 tablespoons diced red onion

1 teaspoon chopped fresh oregano

⅛ teaspoon salt

2 whole wheat tortillas

⅓ cup hummus

½ pound sliced deli turkey breast

1 cup chopped romaine lettuce

1 In a mixing bowl, combine diced cucumber, red onion, oregano, and salt.

2 Lay the 2 tortillas out and spread an equal amount of the hummus in a straight line across each.

3 Top the hummus on each tortilla with an equal amount of the cucumber mixture and then an equal amount of the turkey breast. Finally, cover with half of the lettuce.

4 Roll each tortilla up as tight as possible, seam side down. Slice each in half and serve.

DR. SIEGAL'S TIPS

There are many great flavors of hummus out there. Try these wraps with garlic or roasted red pepper hummus for even more flavor!

300 calories

CALORIES	FAT	PROTEIN	CARBS	FIBER
285	11g	28g	23g	6g

CRANBERRY TUNA SALAD SANDWICHES

PREP TIME: 15 MINS   COOK TIME: 0 MINS   SERVES: 2

Tuna salad is one of the quickest meals to prepare and best sources of protein you can feed your body. This particular recipe is my favorite for tuna salad, as it combines the tangy flavor of Miracle Whip with tart lemon juice and sweetened cranberries. Prepare this in sandwiches for under 300 calories or simply skip step 4 and serve scooped over a bed of lettuce for only 200 calories.

SHOPPING LIST

1 (6-ounce) can solid white tuna

2 tablespoons Miracle Whip Light

2 tablespoons dried sweetened cranberries

2 tablespoons diced celery

¼ teaspoon lemon juice

⅛ teaspoon celery salt

⅛ teaspoon ground mustard

4 slices light wheat bread, toasted

lettuce, to dress

4 slices tomato

1 Drain tuna well.

2 In a mixing bowl, combine Miracle Whip, cranberries, celery, lemon juice, celery salt, and ground mustard.

3 Gently fold the drained tuna into the cranberry and dressing mixture.

4 Top 2 pieces of the wheat toast with several leaves of lettuce to start 2 sandwiches. Top each sandwich with half of the tuna salad. Place 2 slices of tomato on each followed by the top piece of toast to finish the sandwiches. Serve immediately.

DR. SIEGAL'S TIPS

"Light" wheat bread is usually sold in the ordinary bread aisle. It typically has a serving size of 2 slices for the same amount of calories or less than a 1 slice serving of other breads. It's always important to check the serving size! In this case, you get 2 slices of bread for the calories of 1.

300 calories

CALORIES	FAT	PROTEIN	CARBS	FIBER
320	10g	36g	31g	9g

TUSCAN CHICKEN SANDWICHES

PREP TIME: 20 MINS   COOK TIME: 8 MINS   SERVES: 2

Nowadays, nice bakery cafes are proving that sandwiches can be more than just cold cuts and processed cheese. This Tuscan Chicken Sandwich is stuffed with thick slices of real chicken breast and topped with marinated Italian vegetables and my own recipe for a quick and easy Italian Mayonnaise.

SHOPPING LIST

4 slices light wheat bread

thinly sliced red onion

8 ounces cooked chicken breast, sliced into strips

¼ cup shredded mozzarella cheese

1 jarred roasted red pepper, sliced

½ cup marinated artichoke hearts, drained

ITALIAN MAYONNAISE

2 tablespoons low-fat mayonnaise

1 tablespoon grated Parmesan cheese

¼ teaspoon Italian seasoning

⅛ teaspoon garlic powder

1 Start preparing 2 separate sandwiches by topping 2 slices of the light wheat bread with a few thin slices of red onion.

2 If starting with cold chicken, microwave for 1 minute, or until warmed. Place an equal amount over top of the onions on each sandwich.

3 Sprinkle the shredded mozzarella cheese over the chicken on both sandwiches, and then top with a few slices of roasted red pepper and ½ of the marinated artichoke hearts.

4 Spread ½ of the Italian Mayonnaise on each of the top slices of bread and then put in place to finish the sandwiches.

5 Grill on an indoor grill, griddle, or Panini press, until the bread is well toasted on both sides. Or brown in a nonstick skillet over medium heat, about 4 minutes on each side.

ITALIAN MAYONNAISE

In a mixing bowl, whisk together all ingredients. For best flavor, cover and refrigerate for 30 minutes before using.

300 calories

Coleslaw
recipe page: 46

CALORIES	FAT	PROTEIN	CARBS	FIBER
330	8g	30g	34g	5g

TURKEY REUBENS

PREP TIME: 5 MINS   COOK TIME: 15 MINS   SERVES: 2

Reubens are a Jewish deli classic that I've loved for as long as I can remember. While the higher-fat, higher-salt corned beef variety is good on a special occasion, this Turkey Reuben recipe is much more suitable for every day. Serve alongside my Coleslaw, recipe page: 46, for a real deli treat!

SHOPPING LIST

nonstick cooking spray
½ pound deli turkey
½ cup sauerkraut
4 slices rye or wheat bread
2 slices reduced-fat Swiss cheese
2 tablespoons fat-free Thousand Island dressing

1 Spray a large skillet with nonstick cooking spray and place over medium heat. Separate turkey into two sandwich sized mounds and place in skillet.

2 Thoroughly drain sauerkraut and top each mound of turkey with a mound of the drained sauerkraut. Cover skillet and let cook 4-5 minutes, just until warmed.

3 Top 2 slices of rye bread with a slice of Swiss cheese. Transfer each warmed turkey and sauerkraut mound over top of the Swiss cheese.

4 Drizzle Thousand Island dressing equally over both mounds of sauerkraut, and then complete each sandwich by topping with the other slice of rye bread.

5 Re-spray the skillet with nonstick cooking spray and add the sandwiches to it, cooking over medium heat for 5 minutes on each side, or until golden brown.

DR. SIEGAL'S TIPS

I like to look for rye or wheat bread that is labeled "light," as it typically has only 40-50 calories a slice and 3-5 grams of fiber as well!

If using real, thick-cut rye bread from the deli (which is much higher in calories than commercial bakery bread), I would suggest serving these sandwiches open-faced, skipping the top piece of bread to keep the calorie count in line.

300 calories

CALORIES	FAT	PROTEIN	CARBS	FIBER
275	7g	13g	31g	11g

BLACK BEAN BURGERS

PREP TIME: 30 MINS   COOK TIME: 10 MINS   SERVES: 4

These Black Bean Burgers are a great low-fat alternative for your next picnic. While veggie or bean burgers are always compared to their ground beef counterparts, I like to judge them in a class of their own—as they are definitely not the same, but really, really good in their own right. Black Bean Burgers are especially creamy on the inside and can even be made into smaller patties and served as an appetizer, much like you would serve crab cakes.

SHOPPING LIST

1 (15-ounce) can black beans, drained
¼ cup all-purpose flour
¼ cup old-fashioned oats
1 large egg white
1 teaspoon lemon juice
1 teaspoon minced garlic
½ teaspoon chili powder
¼ teaspoon onion powder
¼ teaspoon salt
¼ teaspoon pepper
⅓ cup diced yellow onion
¼ cup finely diced red bell pepper
1 tablespoon olive oil
4 wheat hamburger buns

1 In a large mixing bowl, mash black beans until nearly smooth. (A potato masher works best.)

2 Add the flour, oats, egg white, lemon juice, garlic, chili powder, onion powder, salt, and pepper, and mix (with your hands or a heavy spoon) until well combined.

3 Fold yellow onion and red bell pepper into the black bean mixture, cover, and refrigerate for 15 minutes.

4 Heat olive oil in a large skillet over medium to medium-high heat. Use your hands to form the chilled bean mixture into 4 equal sized patties, and place into the skillet.

5 Cook burgers for about 5 minutes on each side, or until they are hot and beginning to brown. Serve on hamburger buns with your favorite burger fixings.

DR. SIEGAL'S TIPS

For spicier burgers, replace the diced red bell pepper with 1 seeded and diced jalapeño pepper.

300 calories

CALORIES	FAT	PROTEIN	CARBS	FIBER
270	3g	37g	22g	0.5g

Apricot Glazed Chicken

PREP TIME: 15 MINS   COOK TIME: 30 MINS   SERVES: 4

Chicken and fruit are a wonderful combination that I don't see enough of these days. This recipe makes a simple marinade out of apricot preserves that you can then boil as the chicken bakes to create a sauce for even more fruit flavor. And if apricots aren't your thing, this recipe works just as good with apple jelly!

Shopping List

½ cup apricot preserves

2 tablespoons reduced-sodium soy sauce

2 teaspoons lemon juice

3 green onions, sliced

½ teaspoon dried thyme

1 pinch crushed red pepper flakes

4 (6-ounce) boneless, skinless chicken breasts

1 In a mixing bowl, whisk together apricot preserves, soy sauce, and lemon juice, and then stir in green onions, thyme, and red pepper flakes.

2 Add chicken breasts to the marinade in the bowl, and toss to coat. Cover and refrigerate for at least 4 hours to marinate.

3 Preheat oven to 375 degrees F and line a sheet pan with aluminum foil.

4 Remove chicken from marinade (reserving marinade) and place on foil lined sheet pan. Bake for 25-30 minutes, flipping halfway through. Slice into a chicken breast to check for doneness before serving.

5 Place reserved marinade in a small sauce pan over medium-high heat, and bring up to a rolling simmer. Let simmer for at least 4 minutes before drizzling over the cooked chicken breasts to serve.

Dr. Siegal's Tips

Try serving topped with fresh chopped apricots to add a brighter color and flavor to the plate.

300 calories

Zesty Lemon Broccoli
recipe page: 47

CALORIES	FAT	PROTEIN	CARBS	FIBER
275	8g	39g	12g	0.5g

CHICKEN PICCATA

PREP TIME: 15 MINS   COOK TIME: 15 MINS   SERVES: 4

Chicken Piccata is one of my favorite dishes, but the typical preparation can include as much as an entire stick of butter in the sauce! My way of making it substitutes chicken broth in place of white wine and only 1 tablespoon of light, trans-fat-free margarine in place of that stick of butter. The real stars of the dish are lemon and capers, so you won't be missing a thing!

SHOPPING LIST

1 ½ pounds chicken breast cutlets

salt and pepper

½ cup flour

1 tablespoon olive oil

juice of 1 small lemon

¾ cup chicken broth

1 shallot, finely chopped

2 tablespoons drained capers

1 tablespoon light (and trans-fat-free) margarine

fresh parsley, for garnish

1 Generously season chicken cutlets with salt and pepper, and then toss in the flour to coat.

2 Add olive oil to a nonstick skillet over medium-high heat. Add chicken cutlets and cook 2-3 minutes on each side, until golden brown.

3 Add lemon juice, chicken broth, and shallot, and continue cooking for 3-4 additional minutes, or until slicing into chicken reveals no pink.

4 Add capers and margarine to the pan and stir until margarine is melted. Serve cutlets drizzled with capers and sauce from the pan and garnished with fresh parsley.

DR. SIEGAL'S TIPS

I like to add a pinch of salt and pepper to the flour before dredging the chicken.

I also like to crack fresh black pepper over the chicken just before serving.

If the sauce evaporates too quickly, add additional chicken stock or water to thin it out. You only need a spoon or two of sauce over each serving, as it packs a kick!

300 calories

Summer Succotash
recipe page: 31

CALORIES	FAT	PROTEIN	CARBS	FIBER
280	8g	48g	6g	0g

ROASTED RED PEPPER CHICKEN BREASTS

PREP TIME: 15 MINS   COOK TIME: 30 MINS   SERVES: 4

Roasted red peppers are one of the most flavorful ingredients you can buy right off the shelf at any grocery store. Sweet and zesty right out of the jar, there's no need to be concerned about spice—roasted red peppers are quite mild. Like roasted red peppers themselves, this chicken breast recipe packs a ton of flavor with a low amount of calories.

SHOPPING LIST

4 large boneless, skinless chicken breasts (8 ounces each)

1 tablespoon olive oil

2 teaspoons jarred minced garlic

½ teaspoon oregano

¼ teaspoon salt

⅛ teaspoon pepper

½ cup fat-free Italian salad dressing

1 jar (6-8 ounces) roasted red peppers, drained and thinly sliced

1 Add chicken breasts, olive oil, minced garlic, oregano, salt, and pepper to a food storage bag, and toss all to combine. Let marinate in the refrigerator for 15 minutes.

2 Preheat oven to 375 degrees F.

3 Remove chicken from marinade and place on a sheet pan. Bake for 25-30 minutes, making sure to slice into a chicken breast to check for doneness.

4 Add salad dressing and roasted red peppers to a small sauce pan over medium heat. Gently heat, just until hot.

5 Serve chicken smothered in roasted red peppers and dressing from the pan.

DR. SIEGAL'S TIPS

For best results, use a fat-free Italian salad dressing that looks somewhat chunky, usually labeled as "zesty" or "robust".

Roasted red peppers are usually sold in jars in the olive section of the grocery store; though, they may also be located in the canned food aisle or even the Italian foods section.

For a great meal, serve with a salad and my Summer Succotash, recipe page: 31.

300 calories

CALORIES	FAT	PROTEIN	CARBS	FIBER
300	15g	40g	2g	0g

PESTO CHICKEN

PREP TIME: 15 MINS   COOK TIME: 30 MINS   SERVES: 4

Typically, pesto is one of the healthiest looking and tasting dishes that you would be surprised to hear is actually loaded with fat and calories! While the fat is usually coming from good sources like olive oil and pine nuts, most recipes use as much as ½ cup of each, which is simply unnecessary. Pesto is such a strong flavor that the modest amounts of olive oil and pine nuts that I use in my recipe are more than enough to make this dish shine!

SHOPPING LIST

nonstick cooking spray

4 (6-ounce) boneless, skinless chicken breasts

salt and pepper

3 tablespoons pine nuts

2 tablespoons olive oil

2 cloves garlic

¼ cup grated Parmesan cheese

1 cup fresh basil leaves

1 teaspoon lemon juice

1 Preheat oven to 375 degrees F. Spray a sheet pan with nonstick cooking spray.

2 Season both sides of the chicken breasts with a pinch of salt and pepper, and place on the greased sheet pan.

3 Add all remaining ingredients to a food processor or strong blender and blend until smooth, about 1 minute.

4 Spread an equal amount of the blended pesto sauce over the top of each chicken breast.

5 Bake for 25-30 minutes. Slice into a chicken breast to check for doneness. Serve garnished with a fresh basil leaf, if desired.

DR. SIEGAL'S TIPS

You can cut nearly 5 grams of fat and over 40 calories out of this recipe by omitting the pine nuts. If you substitute walnut oil in place of the olive oil, you will get a nice nutty flavor that fills the void of those pine nuts quite well.

Spinach Stuffed Chicken Breasts

PREP TIME: 20 MINS   COOK TIME: 20 MINS   SERVES: 2

With so few calories and so many great nutrients and antioxidants, spinach is one of the best foods on the planet. It's only a wonderful coincidence that it goes so well in a vast array of great dishes, such as this recipe for stuffed chicken breasts. Just a small amount of Parmesan cheese is all you need to give the spinach stuffing a rich flavor without a ton of added fat.

Shopping List

2 large boneless, skinless chicken breasts (8 ounces each)

2 teaspoons olive oil

¼ teaspoon salt

⅛ teaspoon black pepper

⅛ teaspoon onion powder

⅛ teaspoon dry oregano

1 cup frozen chopped spinach, thawed and drained

1 tablespoon Parmesan cheese

1 clove garlic, minced

1 Preheat the oven to 400 degrees F. Place chicken breasts between two sheets of plastic wrap and pound with a meat mallet or rolling pin until flattened and about ⅓ inch thick.

2 Place pounded chicken breasts in a mixing bowl and cover with olive oil, salt, pepper, onion powder, and oregano. Toss until chicken is well coated.

3 In another mixing bowl, combine all remaining ingredients to make the stuffing.

4 Place pounded and seasoned chicken breasts on a sheet pan. Spoon ½ of the spinach filling onto each chicken breast and tuck the sides of the breast up and over it.

5 Flip stuffed breasts and place the overlapped side down on the sheet pan to hold itself in place. Bake 20 minutes, or until slicing into one of the breasts reveals no pink. Let cool 5 minutes before serving.

Dr. Siegal's Tips

Once cooled, these can be sliced into perfect, circular slices for a very nice presentation. This takes a really good knife though, as the spinach can be tough to slice through.

This recipe is easily doubled or tripled to feed the entire family without any need to adjust the cooking time.

300 calories

CALORIES	FAT	PROTEIN	CARBS	FIBER
310	15g	36g	8g	0.5g

CRUSTLESS TURKEY SAUSAGE QUICHE

PREP TIME: 15 MINS   COOK TIME: 40 MINS   SERVES: 4

While quiche is often considered a "light" brunch-time meal, it is typically one of the highest fat dishes around! Usually made from a butter-laden crust and filled with whole eggs, several cups of cheese, and as much as 2 cups of heavy cream… a regular sausage quiche could contain as much as 1,000 calories and 80 grams of fat in the same serving size that I've done for 310 calories in my recipe!

SHOPPING LIST

nonstick cooking spray

8 ounces turkey breakfast sausage, chopped

1 (16-ounce) carton egg substitute

2 large eggs

⅓ cup fat-free sour cream

1 tablespoon all-purpose flour

⅛ teaspoon garlic powder

¼ teaspoon salt

⅛ teaspoon pepper

1 cup shredded 2% milk Cheddar cheese

3 green onions, sliced

2 tablespoons diced pimentos

1 Preheat oven to 350 degrees F. Spray an 8x8 baking dish with nonstick cooking spray.

2 In a nonstick skillet over medium-high heat, brown the turkey sausage until entirely cooked. Drain well, and then place in the greased baking dish.

3 In a mixing bowl, whisk together egg substitute, eggs, sour cream, flour, garlic powder, salt, and pepper. Pour over turkey sausage in the baking dish.

4 Add the cheese, green onions, and pimentos to the baking dish, and stir all lightly to combine.

5 Bake 35-40 minutes, or until the center of the quiche is set and springy to the touch. Let cool 5 minutes before slicing.

DR. SIEGAL'S TIPS

If starting with pre-cooked frozen turkey sausage, simply skip the browning in step 2 and microwave according to the package directions instead. Once cooked, chop and add to the baking dish.

300 calories

Orange Snap Peas
recipe page: 40

114

CALORIES	FAT	PROTEIN	CARBS	FIBER
275	6g	48g	9g	0g

HONEY GARLIC CHICKEN

PREP TIME: 10 MINS   COOK TIME: 30 MINS   SERVES: 4

Honey and garlic are complete opposites that most definitely attract. This Asian inspired chicken breast recipe is a new restaurant favorite that can be easily recreated at home with far healthier results. Serve with one of my 100 calorie vegetable recipes and a serving of brown rice for a complete meal.

SHOPPING LIST

4 large boneless, skinless chicken breasts (8 ounces each)

1 tablespoon jarred minced garlic

2 tablespoons honey

2 teaspoons soy sauce

2 teaspoons sesame oil

toasted sesame seeds, for garnish

1 Add chicken breasts, garlic, honey, soy sauce, and sesame oil to a food storage bag, and toss all to combine. Refrigerate for 1 hour to marinate.

2 Preheat oven to 375 degrees F. and line a sheet pan with aluminum foil.

3 Remove chicken from marinade and place on foil lined pan. Bake for 25-30 minutes, flipping halfway through. Slice into a chicken breast to check for doneness.

4 Serve garnished with toasted sesame seeds, if desired.

DR. SIEGAL'S TIPS

Toasting sesame seeds is easy: Simply place raw sesame seeds in a dry skillet over medium heat and swirl them around the pan until they turn golden brown.

This recipe goes great with Orange Snap Peas, recipe page: 40, or Sesame Broccoli and Bell Pepper, recipe page: 41.

300 calories

CALORIES	FAT	PROTEIN	CARBS	FIBER
290	8.5g	40g	8.5g	1g

Apple Cheddar Chicken Breasts

PREP TIME: 25 MINS   COOK TIME: 30 MINS   SERVES: 4

Apples and Cheddar have always been a great cracker combination, so I thought it might be a really good idea to bake them over top chicken. As it turns out… it wasn't a good idea… it was a great one!

Shopping List

4 (6-ounce) boneless, skinless chicken breasts
2 teaspoons olive oil
2 tablespoons finely minced yellow onion
½ teaspoon dried thyme
¼ teaspoon salt
⅛ teaspoon pepper
1 apple, peeled, cored, and diced
3 tablespoons Italian breadcrumbs
1 tablespoon light (and trans-fat free) margarine
½ cup shredded sharp Cheddar cheese

1 Add chicken breasts, olive oil, minced onion, thyme, salt, and pepper to a food storage bag, and toss all to combine. Refrigerate and let marinate for 15 minutes.

2 Preheat oven to 375 degrees F. Remove chicken from marinade and place on a sheet pan.

3 In a mixing bowl, combine diced apple, breadcrumbs, and margarine, and then spoon over top of the chicken breasts.

4 Bake for 25-30 minutes, slicing into a chicken breast to check for doneness.

5 Top chicken breasts with the Cheddar cheese and return to the oven, baking an additional 3-4 minutes, just until cheese has melted. Serve immediately.

Dr. Siegal's Tips

You can also stuff the chicken breasts with the apple and breadcrumb mixture for an even nicer presentation, but you must first use a meat mallet to pound the chicken out until it is about ⅓ inch thick. Marinate the pounded chicken, and then spoon the apple and breadcrumb filling into the center of each. Fold the corners of each chicken breast in and secure with toothpicks before baking. I would still recommend topping with the cheese in step 5 rather than adding it to the stuffing, as cheese almost always oozes out of stuffed chicken as it bakes anyway.

300 calories

CALORIES	FAT	PROTEIN	CARBS	FIBER
265	16g	27g	1g	0.5g

BLACKENED CATFISH

PREP TIME: 10 MINS   COOK TIME: 6 MINS   SERVES: 4

Blackening spice is a great Cajun way to cook up seafood or even chicken. Not too spicy, but bursting with flavor, my recipe is sure to please everyone. In the South, Blackened Catfish is a household staple, but you can use this exact recipe for any type of white fish. Cod and Tilapia are both lower in calories and fat than catfish and work great in this recipe, but I left this as is to make sure that there was a good variety of seafood choices in this book. Sometimes, one fish will just look fresher or be on sale for far cheaper than the others.

SHOPPING LIST

2 teaspoons paprika
½ teaspoon black pepper
¼ teaspoon white pepper
¼ teaspoon ground red (cayenne) pepper
½ teaspoon garlic powder
½ teaspoon salt
½ teaspoon dried thyme
1 ½ pounds catfish fillets
1 tablespoon canola oil
lemon wedges, for garnish

1 In a mixing bowl, combine paprika, black pepper, white pepper, ground red pepper, garlic powder, salt, and thyme to create the blackening spice.

2 Evenly coat both sides of all fillets with the blackening spice.

3 Heat canola oil in a large nonstick skillet over medium-high heat until very hot.

4 Add coated fillets to the skillet and cook for about 3-4 minutes on each side, or until fish is white in the center and easily flaked with a fork. Serve with fresh lemon wedges, if desired.

DR. SIEGAL'S TIPS

Skillet frying with blackening spice can create a lot of smoke, so you will definitely want to keep your overhead exhaust fan on high. Do not be concerned; the fish is not burning.

300 calories

CALORIES	FAT	PROTEIN	CARBS	FIBER
260	5.5g	43g	11g	1g

ISLAND SPICED TILAPIA WITH FRESH MANGO

PREP TIME: 15 MINS   COOK TIME: 15 MINS   SERVES: 4

Tilapia is not only one of the mildest and lowest calorie fish, but also one of the easiest to find. I've found that my local grocery stores have an ever rotating selection of seafood, but tilapia is pretty much always available and at a pretty reasonable price. This recipe with the unique flavors of allspice and cinnamon goes great topped with fresh mango slices.

SHOPPING LIST

1 tablespoon olive oil

2 tablespoons finely minced red onion

1 teaspoon lime juice

2 teaspoons brown sugar

¼ teaspoon dry thyme

⅛ teaspoon ground allspice

⅛ teaspoon ground cinnamon

⅛ teaspoon crushed red pepper flakes

¼ teaspoon salt

⅛ teaspoon black pepper

4 (8-ounce) tilapia fillets

1 mango, peeled and thinly sliced

1 Preheat oven to 375 degrees F.

2 In a large mixing bowl, combine olive oil, minced red onion, lime juice, brown sugar, thyme, allspice, cinnamon, red pepper flakes, salt, and pepper to create a spice rub.

3 Add the tilapia fillets to the spice rub and toss gently to entirely coat. Transfer spice rubbed fillets to a sheet pan.

4 Bake 15 minutes, or until fish is white throughout and easily flaked with a fork. Top each fillet with a few thin slices of mango and serve immediately.

DR. SIEGAL'S TIPS

If you do not like spicy foods, leaving out the crushed red pepper flakes would be recommended.

If you have extra calories in your daily allowance, alternating between fresh mango and avocado slices atop the fish makes for an even better presentation. However, it is important to remember that ¼ of an avocado has 80 calories and 7g of (mostly good) fat.

300 calories

CALORIES	FAT	PROTEIN	CARBS	FIBER
300	8g	39g	14g	0g

BAKED SCALLOPS

PREP TIME: 15 MINS   COOK TIME: 15 MINS   SERVES: 2

Scallops are an absolutely wonderful low-fat source of protein, though their tendency to turn rubbery when improperly cooked usually keeps a lot of people from truly enjoying them. This recipe tops them with a great mix of crushed crackers and seasonings and then keeps them nice and juicy by smothering them in light margarine and lemon juice. Makes 2 large servings, but can easily serve 4 as an appetizer. Or, if feeding the whole family, you can easily double the recipe for 4 large servings; no need to adjust cooking times.

SHOPPING LIST

nonstick cooking spray
1 pound sea scallops
½ cup oyster crackers, crushed
2 tablespoons light (and trans-fat free) margarine, melted
1 tablespoon lemon juice
½ teaspoon Old Bay seasoning
¼ teaspoon paprika
¼ teaspoon garlic powder
⅛ teaspoon salt
⅛ teaspoon pepper

1 Preheat oven to 375 degrees F. Spray an aluminum foil lined sheet pan with nonstick cooking spray.

2 Press one side of each sea scallop into the crushed oyster crackers until the crackers stick. Place the scallops, cracker-side up, on the greased sheet pan.

3 In a small container or gravy boat, combine melted margarine and lemon juice. Drizzle over the top of all coated scallops.

4 In a small bowl, combine Old Bay seasoning, paprika, garlic powder, salt, and pepper, and then sprinkle over the top of all scallops.

5 Bake for 12-15 minutes, or until sides of scallops are white and slightly springy to the touch.

DR. SIEGAL'S TIPS

Saltine or even reduced-fat Ritz crackers can be used in place of the oyster crackers, though the Ritz crackers will add more fat to the final recipe.

CALORIES	FAT	PROTEIN	CARBS	FIBER
280	7g	47g	6g	2g

SPINACH AND ARTICHOKE SMOTHERED TILAPIA

PREP TIME: 15 MINS   COOK TIME: 20 MINS   SERVES: 4

Spinach and artichoke dip is one of America's favorite appetizers, as is evident by its inclusion on pretty much every restaurant menu! Typically, it's pretty high in fat and lacking enough protein to keep you full and satisfied—so I solved both issues with this recipe. By topping tilapia with a low-fat spinach and artichoke spread, you get all the flavors you love with a whole lot more protein.

SHOPPING LIST

nonstick cooking spray

4 (8-ounce) tilapia fillets

juice of ½ lemon

¼ teaspoon salt

⅛ teaspoon pepper

1 cup frozen chopped spinach, thawed

¾ cup marinated artichoke hearts, chopped

¼ cup low-fat mayonnaise

¼ cup grated Parmesan cheese

1 teaspoon minced garlic

1 Preheat oven to 400 degrees F. Spray a sheet pan with nonstick cooking spray.

2 Place tilapia fillets on greased sheet pan, squeeze lemon juice over top all, and then sprinkle evenly with the salt and pepper.

3 Squeeze excess liquid from the thawed spinach and then place spinach in a mixing bowl. Add chopped artichoke hearts, mayonnaise, Parmesan cheese, and minced garlic, and mix to create the spinach and artichoke topping.

4 Spread an equal amount of the spinach and artichoke topping over each tilapia fillet.

5 Bake 15-20 minutes, or until fish is white throughout and easily flaked with a fork.

DR. SIEGAL'S TIPS

I like to add a few diced pimentos into the spinach and artichoke topping. Not too much though, just about a tablespoon to add a little color and flavor.

300 calories

CALORIES	FAT	PROTEIN	CARBS	FIBER
325	11g	39g	16g	1g

OVEN BAKED FISH STICKS

PREP TIME: 20 MINS   COOK TIME: 15 MINS   SERVES: 4

Everybody of every age loves fish sticks, but frozen fish sticks can contain more than 5 grams of fat per stick as they are pre-fried before being frozen. With this recipe, you should be able to get 5 fish sticks per serving, with only a little over 2 grams of fat in each.

SHOPPING LIST

2 tablespoons canola oil

1 ½ pounds cod or tilapia fillets

½ cup whole wheat flour, seasoned with a pinch of salt and pepper

2 large egg whites

¼ cup buttermilk

⅛ teaspoon garlic powder

¼ teaspoon salt

⅛ teaspoon pepper

¾ cup Italian breadcrumbs

¼ cup grated Parmesan cheese

1 Preheat oven to 450 degrees F. Spread canola oil out on a large sheet pan.

2 Slice fish fillets into strips about ¾ inch wide.

3 Set out 3 bowls. Place seasoned whole wheat flour in the first bowl. Whisk together egg whites, buttermilk, garlic powder, salt, and pepper in the second bowl. Combine Italian breadcrumbs and Parmesan cheese in the third bowl.

4 Place oiled sheet pan in the preheated oven for 3 minutes to heat, and then carefully remove pan and begin breading the fish.

5 Bread the fish by lightly dipping the strips in the seasoned flour, then the egg mixture, and then fully coating with the breadcrumb mixture. Lay each fish stick on the hot sheet pan as you finish breading it.

6 Once all fish sticks are breaded, bake for 12-15 minutes, flipping halfway through. Cut into one to ensure that they are white and flaky throughout. Serve immediately.

DR. SIEGAL'S TIPS

Low-calorie tartar sauce is available in most grocery stores now, but you can also make your own by combining ½ cup low-fat mayonnaise, 2 tablespoons no sugar added sweet relish, 2 teaspoons lemon juice, and ¼ teaspoon onion powder.

300 calories

CALORIES	FAT	PROTEIN	CARBS	FIBER
295	6g	53g	3g	0.5g

TOMATO AND BASIL TOPPED COD

PREP TIME: 15 MINS   COOK TIME: 14 MINS   SERVES: 4

Cod, like most whitefish, is a wonderful low-calorie source of protein. Cod is even lower in calories and fat than tilapia—though, they're both pretty darn healthy in the long run! This recipe combines fresh sliced tomatoes with whole basil leaves and Parmesan cheese for a light, Italian inspired entrée.

SHOPPING LIST

1 tablespoon olive oil

juice of ½ lemon

2 teaspoons minced garlic

¼ teaspoon salt

⅛ teaspoon pepper

2 pounds cod fillets

8 fresh basil leaves

2 tomatoes, cut in half and thinly sliced (into half-moons)

2 tablespoons grated Parmesan cheese

1 Preheat oven to 400 degrees F.

2 In a large mixing bowl, combine olive oil, lemon juice, minced garlic, salt, and pepper to create a quick marinade.

3 Add the cod fillets to the marinade and toss gently to entirely coat fish. Transfer coated fillets to a sheet pan.

4 Top each fillet with 2 basil leaves and then 3-4 slices of tomato arranged so that they are slightly overlapping. Sprinkle Parmesan cheese over top tomatoes.

5 Cover with aluminum foil and bake 12-14 minutes, or until fish is white throughout and easily flaked with a fork. Serve immediately.

DR. SIEGAL'S TIPS

You want to cover about 50% of the surface of the fillets with basil leaves, so you may need more or less fresh basil depending on the size of the leaves and the shape of the fish fillets.

2-3 large Roma tomatoes can be used in place of regular tomatoes. Since these are smaller tomatoes, you will not have to cut them in half before slicing.

300 calories

400 calories

POULTRY

Chicken Cordon Bleu **127**

Cranberry Turkey Meatloaf **128**

Honey Mustard Chicken with Sweet Potatoes **129**

Chicken and Pineapple Fried Rice **131**

Chicken Salad Platter with Cantaloupe **133**

Creamy Chicken and Mushrooms **134**

Turkey Kielbasa with Cabbage and Apples **135**

LEAN MEATS

Pork with Drunken Dijon Sauce **137**

Pork Chops with Melon Salsa **138**

BBQ Pork Loin Chops **139**

Scalloped Ham and Potato

Casserole **141**

Ham Steaks with Real Cherry Sauce **143**

Balsamic and Herb Pork Tenderloin **144**

Steak Diane **145**

Steaks with Caramelized Onions **147**

Greek Pork with Cucumber Dill Sauce **149**

SEAFOOD

Shrimp Scampi with Asparagus **151**

Maple Glazed Salmon **153**

Scallops Veracruz **155**

Honey Barbecue Salmon **156**

Green Bean and Tomato Salad
recipe page: 30

POULTRY

CALORIES	FAT	PROTEIN	CARBS	FIBER
410	11g	64g	17g	1.5g

CHICKEN CORDON BLEU

PREP TIME: 15 MINS   COOK TIME: 40 MINS   SERVES: 4

While my version of Chicken Cordon Bleu is definitely not traditional, it is certainly healthier! With ham and Swiss cheese on top and a delicious honey mustard dipping sauce served alongside, this recipe is sure to be a hit with the whole family! You could stuff the chicken breasts if you wish, but that effort doesn't result in any difference in flavor.

SHOPPING LIST

nonstick cooking spray

2 large egg whites

salt and pepper

1 cup Italian breadcrumbs

4 large boneless, skinless chicken breasts

4 slices deli ham

4 slices reduced-fat Swiss cheese

¼ cup Dijon mustard

2 tablespoons low-fat mayonnaise

1 tablespoon honey

1 Preheat oven to 375 degrees F. Spray a sheet pan with nonstick cooking spray.

2 In a mixing bowl, whisk egg whites with a pinch of salt and pepper. Place breadcrumbs in a second bowl.

3 Double bread each chicken breast by first dipping into breadcrumbs, then the egg whites, and then back into the breadcrumbs to fully coat. Place onto the greased sheet pan as you go.

4 Bake 30 minutes, flipping halfway through, before topping each breast with 1 slice each of the ham and Swiss cheese. Bake an additional 5-10 minutes, or until slicing into the chicken at its thickest part reveals no pink.

5 Combine Dijon mustard, mayonnaise, and honey to make a honey mustard dipping sauce to serve alongside the finished chicken breasts.

DR. SIEGAL'S TIPS

For the perfect meal, serve with my Zesty Lemon Broccoli, recipe page: 47. The broccoli has a nice amount of fiber that will fill the lack of fiber in this recipe.

400 calories

CALORIES	FAT	PROTEIN	CARBS	FIBER
380	14g	39g	26g	2.5g

CRANBERRY TURKEY MEATLOAF

PREP TIME: 15 MINS   COOK TIME: 1+ HOUR   SERVES: 4

For years I've made this meatloaf, though I've usually called it Thanksgiving Meatloaf, for obvious reasons! With dried cranberries that plump up and rehydrate as the meatloaf bakes, you get little bites of sweetness here and there. The Dijon mustard and brown sugar topping is also sweet and tangy, mirroring the cranberries inside.

SHOPPING LIST

1 ½ pounds lean ground turkey
2 large egg whites
¼ cup ketchup
½ cup Italian breadcrumbs
⅓ cup dried cranberries
4 green onions, chopped
2 teaspoons Worcestershire sauce
½ teaspoon garlic powder
¾ teaspoon salt
¼ teaspoon pepper
¼ cup Dijon mustard
1 tablespoon light brown sugar

1 Preheat oven to 350 degrees F.

2 In a large mixing bowl, use your hands to combine all ingredients except Dijon mustard and light brown sugar.

3 Press the mixture into a loaf or bread pan.

4 Combine the Dijon mustard and light brown sugar, and spread over top of the loaf.

5 Bake 60-65 minutes, or until the meatloaf reaches an internal temperature of 165 degrees F. Let cool at least 5 minutes before slicing.

DR. SIEGAL'S TIPS

If mustard is not your thing, simply replace the Dijon mustard in the topping with ketchup.

400 calories

CALORIES	FAT	PROTEIN	CARBS	FIBER
410	5.5g	53g	43g	6.5g

HONEY MUSTARD CHICKEN WITH SWEET POTATOES

PREP TIME: 20 MINS   COOK TIME: 45 MINS   SERVES: 4

Everyone knows that honey mustard and chicken go wonderfully together, but when you add sweet potatoes and onions into the mix, you get a really unique and delicious combination of flavors. It's something that is incredibly simple, with only a few ingredients, but is very apt to impress your family or guests.

SHOPPING LIST

nonstick cooking spray

3 cups diced sweet potato

1 yellow onion, diced

salt and pepper

2 pounds boneless, skinless chicken breasts

½ cup Dijon mustard

2 tablespoons orange juice

1 tablespoon honey

1 tablespoon light brown sugar

⅛ teaspoon cinnamon

1 Preheat oven to 425 degrees F. Spray a 13x9 baking dish with nonstick cooking spray.

2 Combine the diced sweet potato and yellow onion, and spread across the bottom of the greased baking dish. Sprinkle with a generous amount of salt and pepper.

3 Place chicken breasts over potatoes.

4 Whisk together Dijon mustard, orange juice, honey, brown sugar, and cinnamon, and pour over chicken breasts in the baking dish.

5 Cover with aluminum foil and bake 20 minutes. Uncover and bake an additional 25 minutes, or until potatoes are tender and chicken is cooked throughout.

DR. SIEGAL'S TIPS

Unless you have a personal preference, there is no need to peel the potatoes before preparing this recipe… in fact, a lot of the best nutrients are in the skin!

400 calories

CALORIES	FAT	PROTEIN	CARBS	FIBER
380	9g	31g	46g	4g

CHICKEN AND PINEAPPLE FRIED RICE

PREP TIME: 15 MINS   COOK TIME: 50 MINS   SERVES: 4

I know that fried rice sounds about as far from low-calorie as you get, but this recipe is an extremely satisfying recreation of the classic Chinese take-out dish with only 380 calories per serving! Adding pineapple chunks into this gives it a real teriyaki-like flavor that goes perfectly with the chicken.

SHOPPING LIST

1 cup dry long grain brown rice

1 tablespoon sesame oil

1 pound boneless, skinless chicken breast, chopped

2 tablespoons light (and trans-fat free) margarine

3 tablespoons low-sodium soy sauce

2 teaspoons minced garlic

1 cup pineapple chunks, drained

1 cup frozen snap peas

½ cup shredded carrots

4 green onions, sliced

1 Add brown rice and 2 ½ cups of tap water to a medium pot with a tight-fitting lid. Place over high heat and bring up to a boil. Reduce heat to low, cover, and let simmer for 45 minutes. Remove from heat.

2 Meanwhile, place sesame oil in a very large skillet or wok over medium-high heat. Add the chopped chicken and sauté until browned, about 5 minutes.

3 Add the cooked rice and all remaining ingredients to the skillet, and stir to combine.

4 Stir fry for 7-10 minutes, or until rice is slightly darker in color and chicken is cooked throughout. Garnish with additional green onions, if desired.

DR. SIEGAL'S TIPS

An even easier way to make perfect brown rice is to add much more water, as if you were boiling pasta, and simply strain the rice through a fine colander after it cooks for 45 minutes. This way, there's no need to worry about the rice absorbing every bit of the liquid.

400 calories

CALORIES	FAT	PROTEIN	CARBS	FIBER
405	15g	50g	24g	3g

CHICKEN SALAD PLATTER WITH CANTALOUPE

PREP TIME: 20 MINS   CHILL TIME: 30 MINS   SERVES: 2

I love chicken salad, but even more specifically, I love a good chicken salad platter! I would much rather eat a gigantic portion of the actual chicken salad over lettuce with sweet cantaloupe wedges than cut that portion in half to make room for the calories in bread! Remember that it's the protein in the chicken that fills you up and keeps you satisfied!

SHOPPING LIST

⅓ cup light Miracle Whip

2 teaspoons Dijon mustard

½ teaspoon celery salt

¼ teaspoon pepper

2 cups chopped cooked chicken

1 stalk celery, diced

2 tablespoons finely diced yellow onion

⅓ cup grapes, halved

2 tablespoons chopped walnuts

4 large leaves romaine lettuce

1 tomato, sliced

½ cantaloupe

1 In a mixing bowl, combine Miracle Whip, Dijon mustard, celery salt, and pepper.

2 Gently fold chicken, celery, yellow onion, grapes, and walnuts into the dressing mixture. Refrigerate for 30 minutes to let the flavors combine.

3 Arrange 2 large romaine lettuce leaves on each of two serving plates. Split the tomato slices equally between the two plates, placing them over top the lettuce leaves.

4 Scoop ½ of the chicken salad onto each plate, over top of the tomatoes.

5 Slice the cantaloupe half into thin wedges and arrange alongside the chicken salad. Serve immediately!

DR. SIEGAL'S TIPS

This makes 2 huge portions of chicken salad that could easily make 4 chicken salad sandwiches if you need a lunch for the whole family. This may sound strange, but try the sandwiches with the cantaloupe wedges inside—it's like a really sweet slice of tomato!

400 calories

CALORIES	FAT	PROTEIN	CARBS	FIBER
400	8g	50g	34g	3.5g

CREAMY CHICKEN AND MUSHROOMS

PREP TIME: 15 MINS   COOK TIME: 20 MINS   SERVES: 4

I love one-pan recipes like this one as they can be thrown together with very little cleanup! With chicken, mushrooms, onions, and peas in a rich and creamy sauce that is reminiscent of Alfredo, you'd have a hard time finding anyone that wouldn't love this.

400 calories

SHOPPING LIST

1 ½ pounds boneless, skinless chicken breasts

⅓ cup whole wheat flour, seasoned with a pinch of salt and pepper

1 tablespoon light (and trans-fat free) margarine

8 ounces sliced mushrooms

1 small yellow onion, thinly sliced

½ cup chicken broth

1 cup frozen peas

⅛ teaspoon garlic powder

1 tablespoon parsley flakes

⅛ teaspoon pepper

16 ounces fat-free sour cream

¼ cup Parmesan cheese

salt to taste

1 Slice chicken breasts into 1 inch wide strips and toss in the seasoned whole wheat flour until lightly coated on all sides.

2 Place margarine in a large skillet over medium-high heat. Add the coated chicken and sauté until lightly browned, about 5 minutes. Remove from the pan and set aside.

3 Add mushrooms and onions to the pan and sauté until softened, about 6 minutes.

4 Return chicken to the pan and then add chicken broth, frozen peas, garlic powder, parsley flakes, and pepper. Reduce heat to medium-low, cover, and let simmer for 5 minutes.

5 Stir in sour cream and Parmesan cheese and let cook an additional 3-4 minutes, or until the sauce is bubbling hot. Add salt to taste and serve.

DR. SIEGAL'S TIPS

For an all-in-one meal, try stirring in 2 cups of cooked brown rice in step 5. This will add about 100 calories per serving, making for a 500 calorie dinner! You start with about ⅔ of a cup of dry brown rice for a yield of 2 cups cooked. You can also purchase the vacuum sealed packages of fully cooked rice in the ordinary rice section now (under the name Ready Rice). These packages are exactly 2 cups already!

CALORIES	FAT	PROTEIN	CARBS	FIBER
355	15g	28g	18g	5g

TURKEY KIELBASA WITH CABBAGE AND APPLES

PREP TIME: 10 MINS   COOK TIME: 23 MINS   SERVES: 3

Kielbasa and cabbage has always been one of my favorite family meals. It's quick and easy—and especially with the addition of apples—delicious! By replacing regular kielbasa with turkey kielbasa, you can eat ⅓ of this massive dish and only take in 355 calories! If you're feeding a family of four (which you can definitely do with this recipe) the calorie count goes all the way down to 266!

SHOPPING LIST

1 tablespoon light (and trans-fat free) margarine

1 pound turkey kielbasa, sliced into ⅓ inch thick discs

1 bag (16 ounces) shredded coleslaw cabbage

1 apple, peeled and julienned

¼ cup apple juice

1 tablespoon cider vinegar

¼ teaspoon celery salt

⅛ teaspoon coriander

⅛ teaspoon onion powder

⅛ teaspoon pepper

1 Place margarine in a large skillet over medium-high heat.

2 Add sliced turkey kielbasa to the skillet and sauté until browned, about 8 minutes.

3 Add all remaining ingredients and stir to combine.

4 Lower heat to medium-low and sauté for 10-15 minutes, or until cabbage has cooked down and apples are crisp-tender.

DR. SIEGAL'S TIPS

I highly suggest the cabbage as it is full of the fiber that your body needs to digest food, but if cabbage isn't your thing, you can substitute 1 thinly sliced yellow onion. Or try making this with both the cabbage and the yellow onion—it adds less than 20 calories per serving!

400 calories

CALORIES	FAT	PROTEIN	CARBS	FIBER
400	11g	62g	6g	0g

PORK WITH DRUNKEN DIJON SAUCE

PREP TIME: 10 MINS   COOK TIME: 30 MINS   SERVES: 4

Beer, mustard, and pork are three things that everybody knows go well together… but few would imagine that they could go well together in a healthy way! With a huge portion of 8 ounces of sliced pork tenderloin, smothered in a creamy beer and Dijon sauce, somehow this recipe still manages to come in at only 400 calories and 11 grams of fat.

SHOPPING LIST

1 tablespoon olive oil

2 pork tenderloins (1 pound each)

¼ teaspoon garlic powder

¼ teaspoon salt

⅛ teaspoon pepper

2 shallots, diced

¾ cup light beer

1 tablespoon Dijon Mustard

½ cup fat-free evaporated milk

1 Preheat oven to 450 degrees F. Add olive oil to a large skillet over medium-high heat.

2 Sprinkle all sides of the pork tenderloins with the garlic powder, salt, and pepper.

3 Add tenderloins to the skillet and lightly brown each on all sides, about 6 minutes. Transfer to a sheet pan and bake 12-15 minutes, or until a meat thermometer registers 160 degrees. Remove from oven and let rest 10 minutes before carving.

4 Meanwhile, add the shallots to the same skillet you browned the tenderloins in. Once they are sizzling, add the beer and let boil for 5 minutes, or until the liquid has reduced by half.

5 Reduce heat to medium-low and whisk in Dijon mustard and evaporated milk. Let simmer 2-3 minutes before serving over the sliced pork tenderloin.

DR. SIEGAL'S TIPS

All of the alcohol in the beer cooks out as the sauce simmers, but if you would prefer, this can also be made with chicken stock in place of the beer.

400 calories

PORK CHOPS WITH MELON SALSA

PREP TIME: 20 MINS   COOK TIME: 17 MINS   SERVES: 4

The cooling and sweet cantaloupe salsa in this recipe makes the perfect accompaniment to the spicy, Cajun seasoned boneless pork loin chops. While the recipe calls for cantaloupe to make the salsa, you can also use honeydew melon or even a combination of the two.

400 calories

SHOPPING LIST

½ teaspoon paprika
½ teaspoon salt
¼ teaspoon pepper
¼ teaspoon garlic powder
⅛ teaspoon ground red (cayenne) pepper
¼ teaspoon thyme
2 pounds boneless pork loin chops
1 tablespoon olive oil

SALSA

1 ½ cups diced cantaloupe
1 tomato, diced
½ cup diced green bell pepper
¼ cup diced red onion
½ teaspoon minced garlic
juice of ½ lime
1 tablespoon chopped fresh cilantro
salt and pepper

1 Preheat oven to 400 degrees F. Combine paprika, salt, pepper, garlic powder, ground red pepper, and thyme, and sprinkle over both sides of the pork loin chops.

2 Place olive oil in a large skillet over medium-high heat and heat for 1 minute.

3 Add seasoned pork chops to the skillet and brown on both sides, about 3 minutes per side. Remove and transfer to a sheet pan. Bake until pork chops are white throughout, about 10 minutes.

4 Meanwhile, combine all salsa ingredients in a large mixing bowl, and add salt and pepper to taste.

5 Serve pork chops smothered with the melon salsa and a sprig of fresh cilantro for garnish.

DR. SIEGAL'S TIPS

If you like spicier salsas, simply substitute 1 seeded and chopped jalapeño in place of the diced green bell pepper.

CALORIES	FAT	PROTEIN	CARBS	FIBER
370	13g	42g	13g	0g

BBQ PORK LOIN CHOPS

PREP TIME: 15 MINS   COOK TIME: 20 MINS   SERVES: 4

Pork loin chops are some of the leanest and most satisfying cuts of meat you can buy. If you brown them in a skillet before baking them, as you do in this recipe, you can really bring out a lot more flavor than simply baking alone. Adding sautéed red onions, orange juice, garlic, and Dijon mustard to store-bought barbecue sauce gives these an incredible depth of flavor with a very minimal amount of effort.

SHOPPING LIST

2 pounds boneless pork loin chops

salt and pepper

1 tablespoon olive oil

¼ cup diced red onion

¼ cup orange juice

¼ teaspoon garlic powder

1 teaspoon Dijon mustard

½ cup barbecue sauce

1 Preheat oven to 400 degrees F. Line a sheet pan with aluminum foil. Sprinkle pork loin chops with a generous amount of salt and pepper.

2 Place olive oil in a large skillet over medium-high heat and heat for 1 minute.

3 Add seasoned pork chops to the skillet and brown on both sides, about 3 minutes per side. Remove and transfer to the foil lined sheet pan.

4 Add diced onion to the skillet you cooked the pork in and sauté for 2 minutes, just until it turns translucent. Pour orange juice into skillet and use a spatula to scrape any glaze left from the pork from the bottom of the pan. Let simmer 2 minutes.

5 Remove skillet from heat and stir in garlic powder, Dijon mustard, and barbecue sauce. Pour over all pork chops on the sheet pan.

6 Bake until pork chops are white throughout, about 10 minutes.

DR. SIEGAL'S TIPS

Most pork loin chops sold in grocery stores are well-trimmed of excess fat, but if yours are not, I would recommend using a sharp knife to trim them yourself.

400 calories

CALORIES	FAT	PROTEIN	CARBS	FIBER
410	11g	25g	53g	7.5g

SCALLOPED HAM AND POTATO CASSEROLE

PREP TIME: 30 MINS   COOK TIME: 1 ½ HRS   SERVES: 4

While scalloped potatoes with ham and cheese might seem like the farthest thing from healthy, this recipe is actually pretty well balanced. I've used lower fat ingredients to lighten the calorie load, but the real secret ingredient is broccoli! Adding broccoli into the mix not only gives this the flavor of broccoli and cheese soup, but adds a healthy amount of fiber to boot.

SHOPPING LIST

nonstick cooking spray
½ cup chopped yellow onion
3 large potatoes, thinly sliced
8 ounces cubed ham
1 cup chopped broccoli
2 tablespoons all-purpose flour
¼ teaspoon salt
⅛ teaspoon pepper
1 (12-ounce) can fat-free evaporated milk
2 tablespoons light (and trans-fat free) margarine, melted
½ cup shredded 2% milk Cheddar cheese

1 Preheat oven to 325 degrees F. Spray an 8x8 baking dish with nonstick cooking spray.

2 In a nonstick skillet over medium heat, sauté the onion until translucent, about 5 minutes.

3 Place half of the sliced potatoes in the greased baking dish, and top with the sautéed onion. Place ham and broccoli over top of that.

4 Whisk flour, salt, and pepper into the evaporated milk, and pour half over top of the ingredients in the baking dish. Top with the remaining potato slices, and pour remaining evaporated milk over top all.

5 Pour melted margarine over casserole, cover with aluminum foil, and bake 1 hour.

6 Remove aluminum foil, top with Cheddar cheese, and bake an additional 30 minutes, or until potatoes are tender. Let cool 5 minutes before serving.

DR. SIEGAL'S TIPS

Unless you have a personal preference, there is no need to peel the potatoes before preparing this recipe… in fact, a lot of the best nutrients are in the skin!

400 calories

Green Beans with Turkey Bacon
recipe page: 38

CALORIES	FAT	PROTEIN	CARBS	FIBER
370	15g	38g	18g	4g

HAM STEAKS WITH REAL CHERRY SAUCE

PREP TIME: 5 MINS   COOK TIME: 20 MINS   SERVES: 4

Everybody loves a cherry sauce or glaze with ham, but I have never seen one that is made from real cherries! Usually made with canned cherry pie filling or a jar of maraschino cherries, I opted for real, frozen cherries instead. The results might not be the neon red color you're expecting, but the taste is nothing short of delicious! Adding the Dijon mustard to the sauce adds a dimension of flavor that tastes like you used far more than 4 ingredients.

SHOPPING LIST

1 cup frozen cherries

½ cup orange juice

1 tablespoon light brown sugar

1 tablespoon Dijon mustard

2 pounds lean, thick-cut ham steaks

1 Add frozen cherries, orange juice, and brown sugar to a sauce pot over medium heat. Bring up to a simmer.

2 Let mixture simmer for 5 minutes before using a potato masher or heavy spoon to mash cherries into the sauce. Let simmer an additional 5 minutes. Remove from heat and stir in Dijon mustard.

3 Grill, broil, or pan-fry ham steaks (see below) and serve drizzled with the cherry sauce.

GRILLING HAM STEAKS

Oil and preheat a grill, indoor grill, or grill pan to medium-high. Grill ham steaks 3-5 minutes on each side, just until well-marked and hot throughout.

BROILING HAM STEAKS

Set oven rack about 4 inches from the broiler and preheat broiler to high. Place ham steaks on a heavy sheet pan and broil for 4 minutes. Flip steaks and broil 4 minutes on the opposite side.

PAN-FRYING HAM STEAKS

Heat a large nonstick skillet or griddle over medium-high heat for 1 minute. Place ham steaks in the preheated skillet and cook 5-6 minutes on each side, just until hot throughout. You may need to do this in 2 batches to cook all of the ham steaks.

400 calories

CALORIES	FAT	PROTEIN	CARBS	FIBER
360	11g	59g	1g	0g

BALSAMIC AND HERB PORK TENDERLOIN

PREP TIME: 15 MINS   COOK TIME: 20 MINS   SERVES: 4

Rosemary and pork are a timeless combination that is only elevated by the sweet and tart flavors of balsamic vinegar in this recipe. By using the extremely lean tenderloin of the pork, you are able to eat a large 8 ounce portion in only 360 calories. Thinly carved into medallions after roasting, you'd be surprised at just how much 8 ounces is!

SHOPPING LIST

1 tablespoon olive oil

2 tablespoons balsamic vinegar

2 teaspoons minced garlic

2 teaspoons chopped fresh rosemary

¼ teaspoon salt

¼ teaspoon pepper

2 pork tenderloins (1 pound each)

1 Preheat oven to 450 degrees F. Line a sheet pan with aluminum foil.

2 In a large mixing bowl, combine olive oil, balsamic vinegar, garlic, rosemary, salt, and pepper.

3 Add pork tenderloins to the bowl and toss until both tenderloins are coated with the mixture on all sides. Transfer coated tenderloins to the lined sheet pan.

4 Bake 15-20 minutes, or until a meat thermometer registers 160 degrees. Let rest 10 minutes before carving into thin medallions.

DR. SIEGAL'S TIPS

Rosemary has to be one of the most beautiful garnishes you can use, so try garnishing the whole tenderloins with sprigs of fresh rosemary before bringing to the table to slice.

400 calories

CALORIES	FAT	PROTEIN	CARBS	FIBER
390	13g	56g	5g	1g

STEAK DIANE

PREP TIME: 15 MINS   COOK TIME: 20 MINS   SERVES: 4

Steak Diane has been a favorite restaurant dish for as long as I can remember. It used to be prepared right at your table by the waiter! My version uses more inexpensive top sirloin in place of the more traditional filet mignon, but feel free to use the filet if you prefer. They are both pretty lean as far as beef goes.

SHOPPING LIST

nonstick cooking spray

1 ½ pounds top sirloin steak, cut into 4 portions

salt and pepper

1 shallot, diced

1 pound button mushrooms, sliced

¼ cup brandy (may use any red wine instead)

½ cup beef broth

¼ teaspoon dry thyme

⅛ teaspoon garlic powder

⅛ teaspoon onion powder

2 tablespoons light (and trans-fat free) margarine

1 teaspoon Dijon mustard

1 Generously spray a large skillet with nonstick cooking spray and place over medium-high heat.

2 Sprinkle both sides of the sirloin steaks with salt and pepper, and place in the hot skillet. For medium steaks, cook about 4 minutes on each side. Transfer steaks to a plate.

3 Add shallots and mushrooms to the hot pan and sauté until mushrooms begin to cook down, about 4 minutes.

4 Add the brandy, beef broth, thyme, garlic powder, and onion powder, and bring up to a boil. Reduce heat to medium and let simmer 5 minutes.

5 Remove from heat and stir in margarine and Dijon mustard. Season the sauce with salt and pepper to taste. Return steaks to the pan to coat in the sauce and then immediately transfer to serving plates. Serve smothered with mushrooms and sauce from the pan.

DR. SIEGAL'S TIPS

For a creamier sauce, try substituting ¼ cup of fat-free sour cream in place of the margarine in step 5.

400 calories

Wedge Salad with
Blue Cheese Dressing
recipe page: 25

CALORIES	FAT	PROTEIN	CARBS	FIBER
360	13g	52g	5.5g	1g

STEAKS WITH CARAMELIZED ONIONS

PREP TIME: 15 MINS   COOK TIME: 20 MINS   SERVES: 4

Well caramelized yellow onions (especially Vidalia) make the perfect topping for a good cut of beef. The acidity of the balsamic vinegar in this dish all but disappears when it cooks with the sugars of the onions, creating a rich, sweet glaze that literally coats the steak.

SHOPPING LIST

nonstick cooking spray

1 ½ pounds top sirloin steak, cut into 4 portions

salt and pepper

2 tablespoons light (and trans-fat free) margarine

2 yellow onions, thinly sliced

1 tablespoon balsamic vinegar

1 teaspoon minced garlic

¼ teaspoon salt

⅛ teaspoon pepper

1 Generously spray a large skillet with nonstick cooking spray and place over medium-high heat.

2 Sprinkle both sides of the sirloin steaks with salt and pepper, and place in the hot skillet. For medium steaks, cook about 4 minutes on each side. Transfer steaks to a plate.

3 Reduce heat to medium and add margarine and onions to the hot pan. Sauté until onions begin to caramelize, about 6 minutes.

4 Add the balsamic vinegar, garlic, salt, and pepper, and continue sautéing an additional 5 minutes, or until onions have fully caramelized.

5 Remove from heat and return steaks to the pan for 15 seconds, tossing with the onions, just to quickly reheat. Serve steaks smothered in the onions.

DR. SIEGAL'S TIPS

For a heartier, zestier flavor, you can substitute 2 teaspoons of Worcestershire sauce in place of the balsamic vinegar in step 4. Or try adding 1 teaspoon of Worcestershire sauce in addition to the tablespoon of balsamic vinegar.

400 calories

Brussels Sprouts with
Caramelized Onions
recipe page: 39

CALORIES	FAT	PROTEIN	CARBS	FIBER
370	14g	45g	10g	0g

GREEK PORK WITH CUCUMBER DILL SAUCE

PREP TIME: 1 HOUR   COOK TIME: 20 MINS   SERVES: 4

With the flavors of lemon and oregano, these pork chops are prepared in the style of a classic Greek dish called Pork Souvlaki. The Cucumber Dill Sauce is an easier and healthier version of a classic Greek tzatziki sauce.

SHOPPING LIST

2 pounds boneless pork loin chops
1 tablespoon olive oil
1 tablespoon lemon juice
½ teaspoon lemon zest
1 teaspoon dry oregano
1 teaspoon minced garlic
¼ teaspoon salt
⅛ teaspoon pepper

CUCUMBER DILL SAUCE

⅓ of 1 cucumber, peeled
8 ounces fat-free sour cream
1 tablespoon fresh chopped dill
1 teaspoon minced garlic
¼ teaspoon onion powder
⅛ teaspoon salt
⅛ teaspoon pepper

1 Add pork chops to a large bowl, and add olive oil, lemon juice, lemon zest, oregano, garlic, salt, and pepper. Toss to fully coat, cover bowl, and refrigerate for 1 hour.

2 Meanwhile, make the Cucumber Dill Sauce. Add the peeled cucumber to a food processor and pulse until finely minced.

3 Transfer the minced cucumber to a bowl and add all remaining sauce ingredients. Stir well, cover, and refrigerate for at least 1 hour.

4 Grill or pan-fry the marinated pork chops (see below) and serve with Cucumber Dill Sauce.

GRILLING PORK CHOPS

Oil and preheat a grill, indoor grill, or grill pan to medium-high. Grill pork chops until mostly white throughout. Thin chops (¼-inch thick) should take 3-4 minutes on each side to cook. Thick chops (¾-inch thick) should take about 10 minutes on each side.

PAN-FRYING PORK CHOPS

Place chops in a large skillet over medium-high heat. Cook 3-4 minutes on each side, until browned. Thin chops (¼-inch thick) should be done at this point. For thick chops (¾-inch thick), you should transfer the browned chops to an oven preheated at 400 degrees F. and bake 10 minutes, or until chops are mostly white throughout.

400 calories

CALORIES	FAT	PROTEIN	CARBS	FIBER
430	10g	45g	39g	6g

SHRIMP SCAMPI WITH ASPARAGUS

PREP TIME: 15 MINS   COOK TIME: 45 MINS   SERVES: 4

Shrimp Scampi is a classic seafood dish with the great flavors of butter, lemon, garlic, and white wine. Of course, to make things healthier, I substitute light margarine in place of the butter and toss in whole wheat linguine in place of regular, white pasta. My best change of all… adding a whole pound of fresh asparagus!

SHOPPING LIST

1 pound asparagus, stalks trimmed

6 ounces whole wheat linguine

2 teaspoons olive oil

1 ½ pounds shrimp, peeled

2 shallots, finely diced

3 tablespoons light (and trans-fat free) margarine

¼ cup white wine

1 tablespoon minced garlic

juice of 1 lemon

½ teaspoon salt

¼ teaspoon pepper

fresh chopped parsley

2 tablespoons grated Parmesan cheese

1 Boil asparagus for 3-5 minutes, just until crisp tender. Drain and rinse under cold water.

2 Boil whole wheat linguine according to the directions on the box. Drain and rinse under cold water.

3 Meanwhile, place olive oil in a large skillet over medium-high heat. Add the shrimp and shallots, and sauté for 3 minutes.

4 Add the cooked asparagus, cooked linguine, margarine, white wine, garlic, lemon juice, salt, and pepper, and sauté all together for 2 additional minutes, or until shrimp are mostly white throughout.

5 Serve garnished with fresh chopped parsley and a sprinkling of grated Parmesan cheese.

DR. SIEGAL'S TIPS

If using frozen shrimp, be sure to buy raw shrimp and not fully-cooked cocktail shrimp. Let frozen shrimp thaw before preparing.

400 calories

Sesame Broccoli and Bell Pepper
recipe page: 41

Maple Glazed Salmon

PREP TIME: 15 MINS   COOK TIME: 16 MINS   SERVES: 4

Real, natural maple syrup is becoming quite a rarity in homes today, but the difference in flavor (and nutrition) is well worth the premium price, especially when paired with salmon in this satisfying dish! The cheaper maple flavored syrups that are more popular these days are nothing more than flavored high-fructose corn syrup, and I certainly wouldn't recommend using them for this recipe.

Shopping List

1 ½ pounds salmon, cut into 4 fillets

1 tablespoon light (and trans-fat free) margarine, melted

¼ cup natural maple syrup

1 tablespoon low-sodium soy sauce

1 teaspoon cornstarch

1 teaspoon Dijon mustard

⅛ teaspoon ground ginger

1 Preheat oven to 400 degrees F. Place salmon fillets on an aluminum foil lined sheet pan.

2 In a small sauce pan over medium-high heat, whisk together all remaining ingredients to create a maple glaze. Bring up to a simmer and cook for 2 minutes, just until the cornstarch has thickened.

3 Pour an equal amount of the maple glaze over each salmon fillet.

4 Bake 12-16 minutes, or until salmon is opaque and easily flaked with a fork. Serve immediately.

Dr. Siegal's Tips

The aluminum foil is absolutely necessary when baking this recipe as the maple syrup in the glaze will really bubble up and brown. Maple syrup makes for quite a delicious dish, but it is definitely not something that you want to scrub off the bottom of your sheet pan.

400 calories

CALORIES	FAT	PROTEIN	CARBS	FIBER
360	14g	40g	17g	5.5g

SCALLOPS VERACRUZ

PREP TIME: 25 MINS   COOK TIME: 17 MINS   SERVES: 4

This Mexican scallop recipe is my take on a very popular way of preparing seafood that originated in the city of Veracruz. Sometimes made with capers, I make my version with green and black olives and top it with fresh chopped avocado to cut through the slightly spicy tomato broth.

SHOPPING LIST

1 tablespoon olive oil

1 yellow onion, thinly sliced

½ yellow bell pepper, thinly sliced

1 tablespoon minced garlic

2 tomatoes, diced

2 pounds sea scallops

¼ cup green olives, chopped

¼ cup black olives, chopped

juice of ½ lime

2 tablespoons fresh cilantro

¼ teaspoon crushed red pepper flakes

1 avocado, chopped

1 Heat oil in a large skillet over medium-high heat. Add onions and sauté for 5 minutes.

2 Add yellow bell pepper, garlic, and tomatoes, and sauté for an additional 2 minutes.

3 Add scallops, both types of olives, lime juice, cilantro, and red pepper flakes, and stir to combine.

4 Push scallops toward the bottom of the pan to get them closer to the heat. Let cook 3 minutes.

5 Add ⅓ cup of tap water, stir, cover, and let cook an additional 5-7 minutes, or until scallops are white throughout. Serve topped with the chopped avocado.

DR. SIEGAL'S TIPS

Serving this without the chopped avocado on top will bring the calorie count down to 280 calories per serving. It will also cut the fat grams from 14 to 7, but it is important to remember that avocado fat is good fat!

400 calories

CALORIES	FAT	PROTEIN	CARBS	FIBER
395	21g	38g	12g	0.5g

Honey Barbecue Salmon

PREP TIME: 15 MINS   COOK TIME: 20 MINS   SERVES: 4

Pretty much everyone knows that honey and barbecue are a delicious match, but these wonderful flavors are hardly ever seen with salmon… a fish that is just begging for sweet ingredients to cut its rich fattiness (heart healthy fat). This recipe even includes its own honey barbecue glaze made from only a few pantry staples.

Shopping List

1 ½ pounds salmon, cut into 4 fillets

1 tablespoon olive oil

¼ cup tomato paste

1 tablespoon cider vinegar

2 tablespoons honey

1 teaspoon Worcestershire sauce

2 teaspoons lemon juice

⅛ teaspoon onion powder

⅛ teaspoon pepper

1 Preheat oven to 400 degrees F. Place salmon fillets on an aluminum foil lined sheet pan.

2 In a mixing bowl, whisk together all remaining ingredients to create a honey barbecue glaze.

3 Spread an equal amount of the honey barbecue glaze over each salmon fillet.

4 Bake 15-20 minutes, or until salmon is opaque and easily flaked with a fork. Serve immediately.

Dr. Siegal's Tips

You can also make these in aluminum foil "packets" by wrapping each glazed fillet in its own piece of aluminum foil. This will cook slightly faster and seal in all of the juices at the same time. You should unwrap and check one of the pieces of fish at about 12 minutes into cooking with this method, especially if the fillets are thinner than 1 ½ inches thick.

400 calories

500 calories

CALORIES	FAT	PROTEIN	CARBS	FIBER
455	16g	58g	13g	4g

SENSATIONAL CHEF SALAD

PREP TIME: 20 MINS   COOK TIME: 0 MINS   SERVES: 2

While we all know how to throw a few ingredients into a bowl and make a good salad, we don't always know the nutritional information for that particular combination of ingredients. This recipe makes it really simple to create a massive chef salad with a huge array of ingredients in under 500 calories. Serve it with your favorite low-calorie dressing or with one of my salad dressing recipes listed in the tips below.

SHOPPING LIST

6 ounces chopped lettuce mix

8 ounces cooked chicken breast, chopped

8 ounces cubed ham

½ cup shredded 2% Cheddar cheese

1 cup grape tomatoes

½ cucumber, sliced

½ cup shredded carrots

2 hardboiled eggs, halved

1 Split the lettuce equally between 2 large salad bowls.

2 Top the lettuce in each bowl with an equal amount of all salad ingredients, arranging them in their own sections or rows for best presentation.

3 Serve with your favorite low-calorie salad dressing.

DR. SIEGAL'S TIPS

Nutritional information for this combination of ingredients is figured without any dressing. You can serve this salad with any store-bought salad dressing with 2g of fat or less per serving and the final calorie count will be at or around 500 calories. You can also serve this salad with one of these great salad dressing recipes featured elsewhere in this book:

Blue Cheese Dressing, recipe page: 25

Balsamic Vinaigrette, recipe page: 27

Greek Dressing, recipe page: 69

Caesar Dressing, recipe page: 73

Cobb Dressing, recipe page: 161

500 calories

CALORIES	FAT	PROTEIN	CARBS	FIBER
450	18g	45g	25g	5.5g

TWO SEASONS CHICKEN SALAD

PREP TIME: 20 MINS   CHILL TIME: 30 MINS   SERVES: 2

I call this spinach leaf salad my Two Seasons Chicken Salad because it is drizzled with a vinaigrette made from fresh raspberries, which are at their peak in spring, and topped with dried cranberries, which are freshest in the fall. Of course, dried cranberries don't really have a season at all, do they? Gorgonzola cheese and pecans round out this salad for a wonderful mixture of sweet, tangy, stout, and nutty flavors!

SHOPPING LIST

4 cups fresh spinach leaves

¼ red onion, thinly sliced

12 ounces cooked chicken breast strips

⅔ cup crumbled gorgonzola cheese

½ cup pecan halves

½ cup dried sweetened cranberries

DRESSING

¼ cup fat-free Italian dressing

½ cup fresh raspberries

1 tablespoon light brown sugar

1 Split the spinach leaves equally between 2 large salad bowls.

2 Top the spinach in each bowl with a few slices of red onion.

3 Place chicken strips across the center of each salad, and then sprinkle an equal amount of all remaining salad ingredients around the chicken.

4 Serve topped with raspberry vinaigrette and fresh raspberries for garnish, if desired.

RASPBERRY VINAIGRETTE

Combine all ingredients in the bowl of a food processor or blender and pulse until raspberries are completely blended and dressing is smooth. Cover and refrigerate for 30 minutes to let the flavors combine.

500 calories

CALORIES	FAT	PROTEIN	CARBS	FIBER
515	22g	56g	25g	11g

CHOPPED CHICKEN COBB SALAD

PREP TIME: 30 MINS   COOK TIME: 0 MINS   SERVES: 2

Cobb salads are the epitome of a full "dinner salad" that can definitely fill you up. While Cobb salads come in all shapes and sizes, I like mine with chicken, gorgonzola cheese, turkey bacon, broccoli, onion, tomato, and avocado. With that combination, you get the perfect mix of protein, fiber, and good fats (from the avocado).

SHOPPING LIST

6 ounces chopped lettuce mix
2 (6-ounce) chicken breasts, cooked and chopped
¼ cup crumbled gorgonzola cheese
6 slices turkey bacon, cooked and chopped
1 cup chopped broccoli
4 green onions, chopped
1 large tomato, chopped
1 avocado, chopped

COBB DRESSING

¼ cup fat-free mayonnaise
2 tablespoons red wine vinegar
1 tablespoon water
2 teaspoons Dijon mustard
½ teaspoon Worcestershire sauce
¼ teaspoon garlic powder
⅛ teaspoon celery salt
⅛ teaspoon pepper

1 Split the lettuce equally between 2 large salad bowls.

2 Top the lettuce in each bowl with an equal amount of all salad ingredients, arranging them in their own sections or rows for best presentation.

3 Whisk all dressing ingredients together and pour over salads before serving.

DR. SIEGAL'S TIPS

12 ounces of pre-cooked chicken "short cuts" can be purchased from your grocery store to make this without having to cook chicken from scratch. Personally, I like to grill my own chicken and chill it for 1 hour before adding to the salad.

500 calories

CALORIES	FAT	PROTEIN	CARBS	FIBER
455	20g	40g	30g	9.5g

CARIBBEAN SHRIMP SALAD

PREP TIME: 30 MINS   COOK TIME: 8 MINS   SERVES: 2

This salad is not only big enough for an entire meal, it's interesting enough to keep you coming back to this recipe time and time again. Diced mango and sliced avocado in the salad go beautifully with the grilled shrimp skewers on top.

SHOPPING LIST

bamboo skewers
¾ pound jumbo shrimp, peeled
1 teaspoon olive oil
salt and pepper
6 ounces chopped romaine lettuce
¼ red onion, thinly sliced
½ cup diced tomato
½ cup diced mango
1 avocado

DRESSING

⅓ cup pineapple juice
2 tablespoons Dijon mustard
juice of 1 lime
1 teaspoon sugar
¼ teaspoon dry thyme
¼ teaspoon dry rosemary
⅛ teaspoon cinnamon
¼ teaspoon salt

1 Soak bamboo skewers in water for 30 minutes. Preheat a grill, indoor grill, or grill pan to high. Toss shrimp in the teaspoon of olive oil and thread onto bamboo skewers, 3 per skewer. Sprinkle with a generous amount of salt and pepper.

2 Grill shrimp 3-4 minutes on each side, or until mostly white throughout. Set aside.

3 Split the romaine lettuce equally between 2 large salad bowls. Top the lettuce in each bowl with a few slices of red onion and then half of the tomato and mango.

4 Scoop avocado from its peel and slice into thin slices. Fan a few slices across the center of each salad.

5 Top each salad with half of the warm, grilled shrimp. (Remove from skewers, if desired.) Drizzle each salad with half of the Caribbean dressing, and serve immediately.

CARIBBEAN DRESSING

In a mixing bowl, whisk together all ingredients. Cover and refrigerate for at least 1 hour before assembling salads.

500 calories

CALORIES	FAT	PROTEIN	CARBS	FIBER
530	9g	33g	75g	13g

CHILI-MAC

PREP TIME: 10 MINS   COOK TIME: 40 MINS   SERVES: 4

When I am short on time, canned turkey chili is one of my favorite low-fat sources of protein. This recipe is so easy to throw together, and the results are so hearty, that it may just become a new weeknight staple in your house! Or, for a more advanced version with homemade chili, see my tip below.

SHOPPING LIST

8 ounces whole wheat elbow macaroni

2 (15-ounce) cans turkey chili with beans (Hormel is good)

½ cup fat-free sour cream

1 cup frozen corn kernels

⅓ cup finely diced red onion

¾ cup shredded 2% sharp Cheddar cheese

1 Preheat oven to 375 degrees F.

2 Boil the elbow macaroni for 2 minutes less than the package directions. Drain and return to the pot. (Off of the heat.)

3 Add chili, sour cream, and corn to the macaroni, and stir all to combine.

4 Pour the macaroni and chili mixture into a 2 quart baking dish, and sprinkle diced red onion and then Cheddar cheese over top.

5 Bake 25-30 minutes, just until chili is bubbling and cheese is beginning to brown. Let cool 5 minutes before serving.

DR. SIEGAL'S TIPS

If you prefer something more homemade, you can also make this with half of a batch of my Very Veggie Turkey Chili, recipe page: 93. It will actually reduce the calories in this by about 65 per serving.

500 calories

CALORIES	FAT	PROTEIN	CARBS	FIBER
535	13g	42g	65g	8.5g

Tuna Noodle Skillet

PREP TIME: 15 MINS   COOK TIME: 15 MINS   SERVES: 4

This Tuna Noodle Skillet has all of the things you love about a tuna noodle casserole without any baking or unnecessary cans of condensed soup! I like to add a splash of white wine in place of the lemon juice for a more "grown-up" flavor.

Shopping List

8 ounces whole wheat pasta
2 tablespoons light (and trans-fat free) margarine
8 ounces button mushrooms, sliced
1 small yellow onion, diced
juice of ½ lemon
¼ cup all-purpose flour
2 cups low-fat milk
¼ teaspoon dry thyme
¼ teaspoon garlic powder
¼ teaspoon salt
¼ teaspoon pepper
½ cup grated Parmesan cheese
1 cup frozen peas
2 (6-ounce) cans solid white tuna, drained
7 reduced-fat woven wheat crackers, crumbled

1 Boil the whole wheat pasta according to the package directions as you are cooking the sauce.

2 Meanwhile, place margarine in a large skillet over medium-high heat. Add the mushrooms and onion, and sauté until onion is mostly translucent, about 5 minutes. Squeeze the lemon juice over top all.

3 Whisk the flour into the milk and add to the skillet with the thyme, garlic powder, salt, and pepper. Stir until the sauce is bubbling and thick.

4 Stir Parmesan cheese and peas into the skillet until cheese is completely incorporated. Once incorporated, gently fold tuna fish into the skillet.

5 Drain the whole wheat pasta and add to the skillet, tossing it in the sauce to fully coat. Top all with the crumbled wheat crackers and serve immediately.

Dr. Siegal's Tips

Any whole wheat pasta can be used in this recipe. Whole wheat egg noodles are the perfect choice but they are not always easy to find, so shells, elbows, or spirals will work just fine.

500 calories

CALORIES	FAT	PROTEIN	CARBS	FIBER
460	11g	32g	56g	9.5g

POPEYE PIE

PREP TIME: 30 MINS   COOK TIME: 1 HOUR   SERVES: 4

With a name like the one this recipe has, you know that spinach must be involved somewhere! In this case, I've mixed fresh spinach into sautéed ground turkey to make a healthy filling for a mashed potato topped casserole along the lines of a shepherd's pie.

SHOPPING LIST

3 large potatoes
2 tablespoons light (and trans-fat free) margarine
½ cup fat-free sour cream
¼ teaspoon onion powder
¼ cup grated Parmesan cheese
salt and pepper
1 tablespoon olive oil
2 stalks celery, diced
1 onion, diced
1 pound lean ground turkey breast
8 ounces mushrooms, sliced
2 teaspoons minced garlic
1 teaspoon Worcestershire sauce
¼ teaspoon dry thyme
1 tablespoon all-purpose flour
½ cup beef broth
6 ounces fresh spinach leaves

1 Peel, dice, and then boil potatoes until fork tender, about 7-10 minutes.

2 Use a potato masher to mash margarine, sour cream, onion powder, and Parmesan cheese into the potatoes. Add salt and pepper to taste.

3 Preheat oven to 375 degrees F. Place olive oil in a large skillet over medium-high heat. Add the celery and onion, and sauté until onion is translucent, about 5 minutes.

4 Add the ground turkey, mushrooms, minced garlic, Worcestershire sauce, and thyme to the skillet, and sauté until turkey is browned, about 5 minutes.

5 Whisk the flour into the beef broth and add to the skillet along with the fresh spinach. Stir until spinach has cooked down and the sauce in the pan has thickened somewhat.

6 Pour turkey and spinach mixture into a 2 quart baking dish and evenly spread mashed potato mixture over top. Bake 30 minutes, or until potatoes have lightly browned. Let cool 5 minutes before serving.

500 calories

CHICKEN AND ARUGULA FLATBREAD

PREP TIME: 45 MINS   COOK TIME: 25 MINS   SERVES: 3

Arugula is one of my favorite lettuces, as it adds a great peppery taste to anything you put it with. It also looks beautiful atop an entirely homemade flatbread like this one. While it's a little bit of work to make this from scratch, the effort is very well rewarded.

SHOPPING LIST

1 (.25-ounce) envelope active dry yeast

1 cup warm water

2 cups whole wheat flour

¾ teaspoon salt

1 tablespoon honey

1 tablespoon cornmeal

¾ cup pizza sauce

2 tomatoes, sliced

½ small red onion, thinly sliced

8 ounces cooked chicken, chopped

¼ cup shredded Parmesan cheese

½ teaspoon dry oregano

2 cups arugula

2 teaspoons olive oil

salt and pepper

1 Stir yeast into the warm water, and let sit 15 minutes.

2 In a large mixing bowl, add water and yeast mixture to the whole wheat flour, salt, and honey. Knead with your hands until a ball of dough is formed. Cover with a warm, damp towel and place in a warm place to rise for 30 minutes.

3 Split dough into 3 separate portions and roll each out with a rolling pin until about ¼ inch thin. (The shape that you roll the dough out into is up to you!) Place each on a sheet pan that has been sprinkled with cornmeal.

4 Preheat oven to 375 degrees F. Poke a few air holes in each crust with a fork and then pre-bake 10 minutes.

5 Spread ¼ cup of the pizza sauce over each crust and then top with an equal amount of the sliced tomatoes, red onion, chopped chicken, and Parmesan cheese. Sprinkle oregano over top all and bake an additional 15 minutes, or until crust is crispy.

6 Toss arugula in olive oil and salt and pepper to taste. Top each baked flatbread with a handful of the seasoned arugula, and serve immediately.

500 calories

CALORIES	FAT	PROTEIN	CARBS	FIBER
480	18g	53g	18g	4g

ZUCCHINI AND GROUND TURKEY LASAGNA

PREP TIME: 30 MINS   COOK TIME: 1+ HOUR   SERVES: 4

This ground turkey lasagna recipe has one very unique (and healthy) substitution; thinly sliced zucchini in place of lasagna noodles. Once slow roasted, the zucchini takes on almost the exact same texture of noodles, only without the extra carbohydrates!

SHOPPING LIST

nonstick cooking spray
1 pound extra-lean ground turkey
½ cup diced yellow onion
¾ teaspoon Italian seasoning
¼ teaspoon salt
⅛ teaspoon pepper
2 cups prepared spaghetti sauce
2-3 large zucchini
15 ounces part-skim ricotta cheese
2 egg whites
½ teaspoon dry oregano
2 tablespoons Parmesan cheese
2 teaspoons minced garlic
⅛ teaspoon pepper
1 ½ cups mozzarella cheese

1 Preheat oven to 325 degrees F. Spray a 9x13 inch baking dish with nonstick cooking spray.

2 Spray a large nonstick skillet with nonstick cooking spray and place over medium-high heat. Add the ground turkey, yellow onion, Italian seasoning, salt, and ⅛ teaspoon of pepper, and sauté until meat is browned, about 8 minutes.

3 Spread ½ of the meat mixture over the bottom of the greased baking dish and top with ½ of the spaghetti sauce.

4 Thinly slice the zucchini lengthwise (a mandolin works best for this, but be careful!) and then place a full layer of slices, slightly overlapping, over the sauce in the baking dish.

5 In a mixing bowl, combine ricotta cheese, egg whites, oregano, Parmesan cheese, minced garlic, and ⅛ teaspoon of pepper. Drop dollops of ½ of the mixture over top of the layer of zucchini. Top with ½ of the mozzarella cheese.

6 Repeat all to make another layer by first spreading remaining meat mixture, then sauce, then zucchini, then ricotta mixture, and then finally mozzarella cheese.

7 Cover with foil and bake 45 minutes. Raise oven temperature to 350 degrees F, uncover, and bake an additional 25-30 minutes. Let cool 10 minutes before slicing.

500 calories

CALORIES	FAT	PROTEIN	CARBS	FIBER
480	11g	40g	56g	8g

CHICKEN BURRITO BOWLS

PREP TIME: 20 MINS   COOK TIME: 45 MINS   SERVES: 4

Who says that a burrito has to be wrapped into a burrito at all? As the filling of the burrito is what really counts, I've created this version that you eat with a fork! With cilantro-lime rice, chili-seasoned black beans, chicken, shredded Cheddar cheese, sour cream, and a fresh tomato salsa, this is one big bowl of bold flavors.

SHOPPING LIST

1 cup dry long grain brown rice
1 tablespoon olive oil
juice of ½ lime
1 tablespoon fresh chopped cilantro
salt and pepper
1 (15-ounce) can black beans
¼ teaspoon chili powder
⅛ teaspoon cumin
2 (8-ounce) packages Southwestern seasoned cooked chicken strips
½ cup shredded 2% Cheddar cheese
¼ cup fat-free sour cream

FRESH SALSA

2 tomatoes, diced
¼ cup diced red onion
1 small jalapeño, seeded and diced
juice of ½ lime
2 tablespoons chopped cilantro
¼ teaspoon salt

1 Add brown rice and 2 ½ cups of tap water to a medium pot with a tight-fitting lid. Place over high heat and bring up to a boil. Reduce heat to low, cover, and let simmer for 45 minutes. Remove from heat and stir in olive oil, lime juice, cilantro, and salt and pepper to taste.

2 Meanwhile, place the black beans, chili powder, and cumin in a small sauce pot over medium heat. Cover and let cook until hot and simmering.

3 Microwave the chicken strips for about 2 minutes, just until hot.

4 Create each of 4 burrito bowls by spooning an equal amount of the rice into the bowls and topping with an equal amount of black beans, chicken, shredded cheese, and Fresh Salsa. Top with a dollop of sour cream and serve immediately.

FRESH SALSA

Combine all ingredients, tossing gently to disperse the cilantro and salt throughout. Refrigerate for at least 15 minutes to let the flavors combine.

500 calories

CALORIES	FAT	PROTEIN	CARBS	FIBER
520	13g	46g	57g	4g

CHEESY CHICKEN CASSEROLE

PREP TIME: 15 MINS   COOK TIME: 35 MINS   SERVES: 4

Chicken, cheese, and broccoli seem to have been destined to end up in delicious casseroles together. Of course, when this destiny first came to fruition, no one was thinking about the fat content! While many creamy, cheesy casseroles like this one could have more than 50 grams of fat per serving, my recipe shaves that number down to only 13!

SHOPPING LIST

8 ounces whole wheat spiral (fusilli) pasta

2 tablespoons light (and trans-fat free) margarine

1 pound boneless, skinless chicken breasts, chopped

3 tablespoons all-purpose flour

2 cups low-fat milk

1 chicken bouillon cube

¼ teaspoon white pepper

1 (10-ounce) bag frozen baby broccoli florets

½ cup shredded carrots

1 ¼ cups shredded 2% sharp Cheddar cheese

1 Boil the pasta for 2 minutes less than the package directions. Drain, and transfer to a 2 quart baking dish.

2 Meanwhile, preheat oven to 375 degrees F. Place margarine in a large skillet over medium-high heat. Add the chopped chicken and sauté until browned, about 5 minutes.

3 Whisk the flour into the milk and add to the skillet along with the chicken bouillon cube and white pepper. Stir until the bouillon cube is melted and sauce is bubbling and thick.

4 Stir in broccoli florets, shredded carrots, and half of the Cheddar cheese. Pour over the pasta in the baking dish and lightly stir to combine.

5 Top casserole with the remaining half of the Cheddar cheese, and bake 20 minutes, just until casserole is bubbly hot and cheese is beginning to brown. Let cool 5 minutes before serving.

DR. SIEGAL'S TIPS

1 teaspoon of chicken base (sold in jars near the bouillon cubes) can be used in place of the bouillon cube for the exact same flavor with less of the salt.

500 calories

CALORIES	FAT	PROTEIN	CARBS	FIBER
500	10g	47g	56g	8.5g

TERIYAKI CHICKEN AND VEGETABLE LO MEIN

PREP TIME: 20 MINS   COOK TIME: 30 MINS   SERVES: 4

This Lo Mein is a great all-in-one meal that is very well balanced nutritionally. In making a Chinese noodle stir fry, I find that whole wheat linguine works perfectly when healthfully recreating this dish at home.

SHOPPING LIST

8 ounces whole wheat linguine

1 tablespoon sesame oil

1 ½ pounds boneless, skinless chicken breasts, chopped

1 yellow onion, thinly sliced

1 red bell pepper, julienned

3 tablespoons reduced-sodium teriyaki sauce

½ cup beef broth

½ teaspoon cornstarch

1 teaspoon light brown sugar

2 teaspoons minced garlic

1 (12-ounce) bag frozen baby broccoli florets

2 tablespoons light (and trans-fat free) margarine

¼ teaspoon pepper

1 Boil whole wheat linguine for 2 less minutes than the package directions. Drain and rinse under cold water.

2 Meanwhile, place sesame oil in a very large skillet or wok over medium-high heat. Add the chopped chicken and sauté until browned, about 5 minutes.

3 Add the yellow onion and red bell pepper to the skillet, and stir fry for 4 more minutes.

4 Whisk together teriyaki sauce, beef broth, cornstarch, brown sugar, and minced garlic, and add to the skillet along with the cooked pasta, broccoli, margarine, and pepper.

5 Stir fry for 5-7 more minutes, or until broccoli is hot throughout and sauce is thick, bubbly, and coating everything well.

DR. SIEGAL'S TIPS

A bag of frozen stir fry vegetables can be used in place of the broccoli, yellow onion, and red pepper. Simply skip step 3 and add the frozen veggies when you would have normally added the broccoli in step 4.

500 calories

CALORIES	FAT	PROTEIN	CARBS	FIBER
500	8.5g	51g	52g	9.5g

CHICKEN AND PASTA PRIMAVERA

PREP TIME: 20 MINS   COOK TIME: 20 MINS   SERVES: 4

Primavera is one of my favorite Italian dishes, as it is absolutely overflowing with delicious and colorful fresh vegetables. My version is also abundant in high-protein chicken and high-fiber whole wheat pasta for a complete meal that will definitely fill you up!

SHOPPING LIST

8 ounces whole wheat penne pasta

1 tablespoon olive oil

1 ½ pounds boneless, skinless chicken breast, chopped

1 yellow onion, thinly sliced

1 cup vegetable broth

½ green bell pepper, thinly sliced

2 large yellow squash, thinly sliced

2 teaspoons minced garlic

1 teaspoon Italian seasoning

1 pint grape tomatoes, halved

1 tablespoon light (and trans-fat free) margarine

2 tablespoons fresh chopped parsley

salt and pepper

¼ cup grated Parmesan cheese

1 Boil whole wheat penne pasta according to the package directions as you are preparing the rest of the dish.

2 Meanwhile, place olive oil in a very large skillet over medium-high heat. Add the chopped chicken, and sauté until nearly browned, about 4 minutes.

3 Add the onion to the skillet, and sauté an additional 2 minutes before adding the vegetable broth, bell pepper, yellow squash, garlic, and Italian seasoning. Saute until yellow squash is crisp-tender, about 4 minutes.

4 Drain pasta and add it to the skillet along with the grape tomatoes, margarine, and parsley. Stir to combine all and gently heat tomatoes as the margarine melts.

5 Add salt and pepper to taste and serve each serving topped with a full tablespoon of the Parmesan cheese.

DR. SIEGAL'S TIPS

You can also use a bag of frozen Italian blend vegetables in place of the bell pepper and squash, but for Primavera, I say that fresh is definitely the best way to go!

500 calories

CALORIES	FAT	PROTEIN	CARBS	FIBER
450	11g	39g	46g	7.5g

MOO SHU PORK

PREP TIME: 25 MINS   **COOK TIME: 15 MINS**   **SERVES: 4**

Moo Shu Pork is one of my favorite Chinese take-out dishes, but you can't ever be sure how much oil restaurants are using or how lean their pork is. A stir fry of crunchy vegetables and strips of pork that you wrap up in tortillas to serve, you can almost call this a Chinese burrito! The majority of the calories are in the actual tortilla, so limit yourself to 1 wrap and eat any leftover filling as a traditional stir fry—with a fork or chopsticks.

SHOPPING LIST

1 tablespoon canola oil

1 pound pork tenderloin, cut into thin strips

1 yellow onion, thinly sliced

1 red bell pepper, julienned

8 ounces baby bella mushrooms, sliced

1 (16-ounce) bag shredded coleslaw cabbage

¼ cup hoisin sauce

2 tablespoons reduced-sodium soy sauce

1 tablespoon minced garlic

4 whole wheat tortillas

2 tablespoons hoisin sauce, for serving

1 Place canola oil in a very large skillet or wok over medium-high heat. Add the strips of pork and sauté until browned, about 5 minutes.

2 Add the onion, bell pepper, and mushrooms, and stir fry for 4 minutes.

3 Add the shredded coleslaw cabbage, hoisin sauce, soy sauce, and minced garlic, and stir fry for 5 additional minutes, just until cabbage is cooked down (but still crisp) and pork is cooked throughout.

4 Spread ½ tablespoon of hoisin sauce on each tortilla, and then stuff with a generous amount of the moo shu filling to serve. Serve alongside the remainder of the filling, as there will be plenty left over!

DR. SIEGAL'S TIPS

Hoisin sauce may be unfamiliar to you, but it is actually one of the secret ingredients that Chinese restaurants use to create their unique flavors. It is made from soy and has a sweet and spicy, almost barbecue sauce type flavor. You can usually find it in the Asian foods aisle of your grocery store.

500 calories

CALORIES	FAT	PROTEIN	CARBS	FIBER
495	10g	54g	41g	3.5g

CHUNKY CHICKEN POT PIE

PREP TIME: 15 MINS   COOK TIME: 45 MINS   SERVES: 4

Instead of filling my Chicken Pot Pie with unnecessary potatoes, I've upped the amount of chicken to make a pie that is seriously filling, even when feeding a whole family. With a biscuit-like topping and a creamy sauce made with cream cheese instead of canned soup, this is sure to become a favorite!

SHOPPING LIST

2 tablespoons light (and trans-fat free) margarine

1 ½ pounds boneless, skinless chicken breast, chopped

½ cup diced yellow onion

2 stalks celery, sliced

2 ½ teaspoons cornstarch

1 tablespoon all-purpose flour

1 ½ cups chicken broth

8 ounces fat-free cream cheese

1 ½ cups peas and carrots

½ teaspoon dry thyme

¼ teaspoon garlic powder

¼ teaspoon salt

¼ teaspoon pepper

1 ¼ cups reduced-fat Bisquick

2 tablespoons grated Parmesan cheese

1 cup low-fat milk

1 Preheat oven to 400 degrees F. Place margarine in a large skillet over medium-high heat. Add the chopped chicken and sauté until browned, about 5 minutes.

2 Add the yellow onion and celery to the skillet, and sauté with the chicken for 3 minutes.

3 Whisk the cornstarch and flour into the chicken broth and add to the skillet with the cream cheese. Stir until all cream cheese is melted and sauce is bubbling and thick.

4 Stir in peas and carrots, dry thyme, garlic powder, salt, and pepper, and then transfer all to a 2 quart baking dish.

5 In a mixing bowl, combine Bisquick, Parmesan cheese, and milk to create the pot pie's topping. Pour topping over all in the baking dish. Bake 30 minutes, or until topping is golden brown. Let cool 5 minutes before serving.

DR. SIEGAL'S TIPS

You can also make this dish starting with pre-cooked, leftover chicken by skipping the sautéing in step 1. Use about 3 cups of chopped chicken.

500 calories

CALORIES	FAT	PROTEIN	CARBS	FIBER
530	12g	52g	56g	5g

CHICKEN, BROCCOLI, AND RICE ALFREDO

PREP TIME: 15 MINS   COOK TIME: 1 HOUR   SERVES: 4

This skillet rice dish in a creamy Parmesan cheese sauce actually reminds me more of risotto than Fettuccine Alfredo, but that is not a bad thing! A sprinkling of diced tomatoes and parsley added over top just before serving adds a nice splash of color and freshness to this simple and filling dinner.

SHOPPING LIST

1 cup dry long grain brown rice
2 tablespoons light (and trans-fat free) margarine
1 ¼ pounds boneless, skinless chicken breasts, chopped
½ cup diced yellow onion
¼ cup all-purpose flour
2 cups low-fat milk
1 (10-ounce) bag frozen baby broccoli florets
2 teaspoons minced garlic
¼ teaspoon salt
¼ teaspoon pepper
1 tiny pinch ground nutmeg
½ cup grated Parmesan cheese
2 tomatoes, diced
fresh chopped parsley

1 Add brown rice and 2 ½ cups of tap water to a medium pot with a tight-fitting lid. Place over high heat and bring up to a boil. Reduce heat to low, cover, and let simmer for 45 minutes. Remove from heat and let sit 5 minutes before fluffing with a fork.

2 Meanwhile, place margarine in a large skillet over medium-high heat. Add the chopped chicken and diced onion, and sauté until browned, about 5 minutes.

3 Whisk the flour into the milk and add to the skillet along with the broccoli florets, minced garlic, salt, pepper, and nutmeg. Stir until the sauce is bubbling and thick.

4 Stir Parmesan cheese and cooked rice into the skillet, and sauté an additional 2-3 minutes, just until the broccoli is hot and the chicken is cooked throughout.

5 Serve each bowl topped with plenty of diced tomato and a sprinkling of fresh chopped parsley.

DR. SIEGAL'S TIPS

To cut down on the cooking time, in place of cooking your own rice you can substitute 4 servings of pre-cooked brown rice, usually sold in the grocery store under Uncle Ben's Ready Rice brand.

500 calories

CALORIES	FAT	PROTEIN	CARBS	FIBER
470	10g	46g	48g	14g

BEEF AND BLACK BEAN CHILI

PREP TIME: 25 MINS   COOK TIME: 6+ HRS   SERVES: 4

Chili is one of my favorite all-in-one meals, especially this chili, as the extra lean ground beef and black beans ensure that you are getting all of the protein you will need to stay satisfied and full. This makes 4 HUGE servings that come in at only 470 calories each. If sour cream isn't your thing, feel free to top this with 2 tablespoons of shredded 2% milk sharp Cheddar cheese; you will still come in at under 500 calories a serving.

SHOPPING LIST

1 tablespoon olive oil

1 pound extra-lean ground beef

1 yellow onion, chopped

1 red bell pepper, chopped

2 (15-ounce) cans black beans, drained

1 (15-ounce) can diced tomatoes, with juice

1 cup chunky salsa

¼ cup water

1 teaspoon chili powder

¼ teaspoon cumin

¼ teaspoon crushed red pepper

¼ teaspoon garlic powder

½ teaspoon salt

¼ teaspoon pepper

4 ounces fat-free sour cream

1 Place olive oil and ground beef in a large skillet over medium-high heat and sauté until well browned, about 8 minutes. Drain well.

2 Transfer browned ground beef to a slow cooker, set to low, and cover with all remaining ingredients, except sour cream. Stir all to combine.

3 Cover and cook for 6-8 hours before serving topped with a large dollop of the fat-free sour cream.

DR. SIEGAL'S TIPS

Extra lean ground beef is usually labeled as having a 95/5 beef to fat ratio (meaning only 5% is fat). You may also be able to find 96/4, which is even lower in fat. If you have any trouble locating it, extra lean ground turkey also works well in this recipe.

500 calories

CALORIES	FAT	PROTEIN	CARBS	FIBER
525	6.5g	50g	69g	10g

TEX MEX CHICKEN

PREP TIME: 10 MINS   COOK TIME: 6+ HRS   SERVES: 4

This is one of the easiest recipes in this book! You simply throw a few ingredients into a slow cooker, and a few hours later, you have an amazingly delicious "Tex Mex" meal of chicken, corn, and black beans in a creamy (and a little bit spicy) sauce.

SHOPPING LIST

4 boneless, skinless chicken breasts

1 (15.5-ounce) jar chunky salsa

1 (15-ounce) can black beans, drained

1 cup frozen corn kernels

1 tablespoon fresh chopped cilantro

2 teaspoons chili powder

¼ teaspoon cumin

¼ teaspoon onion powder

1 cup dry long grain brown rice

½ cup fat-free sour cream

salt and pepper

1 Place chicken breasts, salsa, black beans, corn, cilantro, chili powder, cumin, and onion powder in a slow cooker set to low.

2 Cover and cook for 6 hours.

3 Before serving, add brown rice and 2 ½ cups of tap water to a medium pot with a tight-fitting lid. Place over high heat and bring up to a boil. Reduce heat to low, cover, and let simmer for 45 minutes. Remove from heat and let sit 5 minutes before fluffing with a fork.

4 Stir sour cream into the cooked chicken mixture in the slow cooker, and add salt and pepper to taste. Serve over brown rice, garnished with a sprig of cilantro.

DR. SIEGAL'S TIPS

Cilantro is sold in bunches near the parsley in the produce department of your local grocery store. There simply is no suitable dry version to be found in the spice aisle.

500 calories

CALORIES	FAT	PROTEIN	CARBS	FIBER
475	13g	55g	28g	7g

CHICKEN CACCIATORE

PREP TIME: 25 MINS   COOK TIME: 6+ HRS   SERVES: 4

This Italian chicken stew is a real "stew" in the truest sense of the word. Slow cooking for 6 hours not only lets the chicken breasts tenderize, but also combines the wonderful flavors of onion, bell pepper, garlic, wine, and—of course—tomato.

SHOPPING LIST

2 tablespoons olive oil

2 pounds boneless, skinless chicken breasts

2 tablespoons all-purpose flour

salt and pepper

1 red onion, sliced

1 green bell pepper, sliced

1 red bell pepper, sliced

1 (28-ounce) jar prepared spaghetti sauce

½ cup white wine

1 tablespoon minced garlic

¾ teaspoon Italian seasoning

16 ounces button mushrooms, sliced

2 tablespoons capers, drained

fresh basil, for garnish

1 Heat olive oil in a large skillet over medium-high heat.

2 Toss chicken breasts in flour to lightly coat. Sprinkle with a generous amount of salt and pepper, and place in the skillet. Cook for 3-4 minutes on each side, until browned.

3 Transfer browned chicken to a slow cooker set to low, and cover with all remaining ingredients, except mushrooms, capers, and basil.

4 Cover and cook for 6 hours.

5 Add mushrooms and capers, and let cook an additional 30 minutes before serving garnished with fresh basil.

DR. SIEGAL'S TIPS

In a pinch, chopped green olives can be used in place of the capers. Or, you can simply use a chunky olive type of spaghetti sauce, usually available in your local grocery store.

500 calories

CALORIES	FAT	PROTEIN	CARBS	FIBER
500	9g	54g	54g	5.5g

JAMBALAYA

PREP TIME: 20 MINS   COOK TIME: 5+ HRS   SERVES: 4

Jambalaya, a Creole dish, is like a spicy stew of chicken, sausage, and shrimp that you serve over rice. I know I only suggest adding hot sauce to taste, but it's really important that you do add it. A good Jambalaya should be spicy! I like to add at least 2 teaspoons of hot sauce (specifically Tobasco) to mine.

SHOPPING LIST

1 pound boneless, skinless chicken breasts, sliced into strips
8 ounces turkey kielbasa, sliced
2 ¼ cups chicken broth
1 (6-ounce can) tomato paste
2 tomatoes, diced
1 green bell pepper, chopped
2 stalks celery, chopped
1 yellow onion, chopped
1 tablespoon minced garlic
2 teaspoons Italian seasoning
½ teaspoon crushed red pepper flakes
1 cup brown rice
½ pound shrimp, peeled
hot sauce
salt and pepper
fresh parsley

1 Place chicken breast strips, turkey kielbasa, chicken broth, tomato paste, tomatoes, bell pepper, celery, onion, garlic, Italian seasoning, and red pepper flakes in a slow cooker set to low.

2 Cover and cook for about 5 hours.

3 Before serving, add brown rice and 2 ½ cups of tap water to a medium pot with a tight-fitting lid. Place over high heat and bring up to a boil. Reduce heat to low, cover, and let simmer for 45 minutes. Remove from heat and let sit 5 minutes before fluffing with a fork.

4 Stir shrimp into the slow cooker and re-cover, cooking an additional 30 minutes.

5 Add hot sauce, salt, and pepper to the Jambalaya to taste. Serve over brown rice, garnished with a sprig of fresh parsley.

DR. SIEGAL'S TIPS

While Jambalaya is typically served over rice, you can also mix the cooked brown rice right into the pot while adding the shrimp in step 4. The brown rice will get a little softer but will also absorb a lot of the great flavors in the broth.

500 calories

CALORIES	FAT	PROTEIN	CARBS	FIBER
490	16g	46g	40g	17g

SAUSAGE AND LENTIL STEW

PREP TIME: 25 MINS   COOK TIME: 7+ HRS   SERVES: 4

While this recipe makes 4 wonderfully hearty servings of Italian sausage and lentil stew, you can also serve this as 8 smaller, appetizer portions of this recipe that come in at only 245 calories each. Either way, the lentils in this stew add a tremendous amount of fiber that will definitely leave you feeling full!

SHOPPING LIST

nonstick cooking spray

1 pound turkey Italian sausage, sliced

1 yellow onion, diced

2 stalks celery, diced

½ cup shredded carrots

3 tomatoes, diced

1 tablespoon minced garlic

4 cups chicken broth

2 cups water

1 cup dry lentils

2 bay leaves

¼ teaspoon poultry seasoning

¼ teaspoon Italian seasoning

½ teaspoon thyme

¼ teaspoon salt

¼ teaspoon pepper

1 Spray a large skillet with nonstick cooking spray and heat over medium-high heat.

2 Place sliced turkey sausage in skillet and cook 5 minutes, just until browned.

3 Transfer browned sausage to a slow cooker set to low, and cover with all remaining ingredients. Stir to combine.

4 Cover and cook for 7-8 hours. Remove bay leaves before serving.

DR. SIEGAL'S TIPS

This is also good topped with a dollop of fat-free sour cream, much in the same way that you would top chili.

500 calories

RECIPE INDEX

100 Calories

200 Calories

SANFORD SIEGAL, D.O., M.D.

Sanford Siegal, D.O., M.D., is a practicing physician whose South Florida medical practice, Siegal Medical Group, has treated more than 500,000 overweight patients. Although he has achieved notoriety for his books on subjects including high fiber diets, hunger control without drugs, and hypothyroidism, he is best known as the "Cookie Doctor" behind the venerable Dr. Siegal's Cookie Diet weight-loss program and hunger-controlling foods. Dr. Siegal is frequently in the news and has been profiled by dozens of media including Good Morning America, The New York Times, The Today Show, Toronto Globe & Mail, Forbes, and Entertainment Tonight.

OTHER BOOKS BY SANFORD SIEGAL, D.O., M.D. INCLUDE:

Dr. Siegal's Cookie Diet Book (Hyde Park, 2009)

Is Your Thyroid Making You Fat? (Warner Books, 2000)

Hunger Control Without Drugs (Macmillan, 1985)

FOR MORE INFORMATION ON DR. SIEGAL AND DR. SIEGAL'S COOKIE DIET, PLEASE VISIT:

WWW.COOKIEDIET.COM